How to Win Chess Endgames

The Secret to Winning Endgames Using Any Combination of Pieces

BILL ROBERTIE

ABOUT THE AUTHOR

Bill Robertie is a chess master and a former winner of the US Chess Speed Championships. He is also a champion backgammon player and a two-time winner of the Monte Carlo World Championships. Besides authoring several books on chess, he's written seven books on backgammon and is the co-publisher of Inside Backgammon, the world's foremost backgammon magazine.

His club and tournament winnings from chess and backgammon allow Robertie to travel the world in style. He currently makes his home in Arlington, Massachusetts.

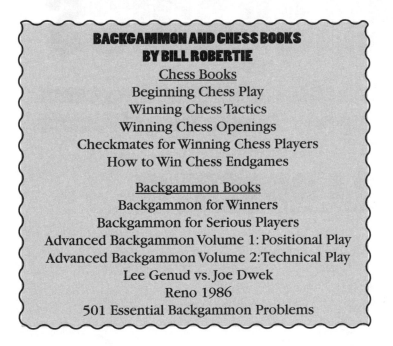

BACKGAMMON AND CHESS BOOKS
BY BILL ROBERTIE

Chess Books
Beginning Chess Play
Winning Chess Tactics
Winning Chess Openings
Checkmates for Winning Chess Players
How to Win Chess Endgames

Backgammon Books
Backgammon for Winners
Backgammon for Serious Players
Advanced Backgammon Volume 1: Positional Play
Advanced Backgammon Volume 2: Technical Play
Lee Genud vs. Joe Dwek
Reno 1986
501 Essential Backgammon Problems

How to Win Chess Endgames

The Secret to Winning Endgames Using Any Combination of Pieces

BILL ROBERTIE

Cardoza Publishing

Cardoza Publishing is the foremost gaming publisher in the world, with a library of mre than 200 up-to-date and easy-to-read books and strategies. These authoritative works are written by the top experts in their fields and, with more than 10,000,000 books in print, represent the best-selling and most popular gaming books anywhere.

Library of Congress Catalog Card No: 2018957788
ISBN: 978-1-58042-360-1

CARDOZA PUBLISHING
(800) 577-WINS • email: cardozabooks@aol.com
www.cardozabooks.com

Write for your <u>free</u> catalogue of gaming books,
advanced strategies and computer games.

TABLE OF CONTENTS

1

INTRODUCTION

When you first start playing and studying chess, many of your wins will be quick and decisive. Your knowledge of tactics and attacking play is enough to overwhelm your inexperienced opponents. Most of your wins come in the middle game or even the opening, as you're easily able to win your opponent's pieces and fashion quick checkmates.

FIRST WORD

It's a lot of fun to win a chess game in the early stages, but it doesn't always happen that way. Sometimes your opponent will match you move for move and idea for idea.

But as you move up the competitive ladder, it doesn't always work that way. Sometimes your more experienced opponents beat off your attacks or, too many pieces get traded for either side to contemplate a quick checkmate. When this occurs, you might not be able to win very much material in the middle stages of the game. What then?

That's when you need to know how to win in the endgame. In the endgame, material has been reduced to the last few pieces and pawns. The game revolves around the struggle to queen those pawns and then win with an extra queen. A skilled endgame player has a big advantage when the game reaches this stage. He can turn an apparently even position into an easy win, or avoid a loss in a game that looked hopeless. In this book, I'll show you how to squeeze out victory in endgames involving kings, pawns, bishops, knights, queens, and rooks. With the lessons you'll learn here, you'll be the player setting the traps, and your opponents will be turning over their kings in surrender.

Let's get started!

2

CHESS NOTATION

By learning chess notation, you'll be able to follow the games and explanations in this or any other chess book. It's really quite easy. Here's how it works.

FIRST WORD
Chess notation is a simplified way of recording the moves in a chess game. It's really quite easy to learn.

Chess notation starts by putting a coordinate grid over the chessboard. Take a look at the diagram below.

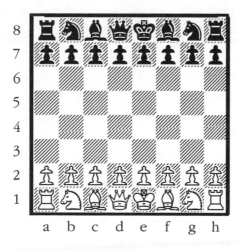

Diagram 1: The notation system

THE NOTATION SYSTEM

The horizontal rows, or ranks, are numbered from 1 to 8. White's first row, the rank containing the White pieces, is number 1. The rank with Black's pieces is now number 8. The vertical rows, or files, are lettered "a" through "h", with "a" starting on White's left and "h" on White's right.

This grid system lets us refer to any square on the board by a unique name. White's king is currently sitting on the square "e1". Black's queen is on square "d8", and so on. In addition to the grid system, there are abbreviations for each of the pieces. Here they are:

BBREVIATIONS FOR THE PIECES	
King	K
Queen	Q
Rook	R
Bishop	B
Knight	N
Pawn	-

To indicate a move, we write down the piece that moved and the starting and ending squares of the move. If a pawn is moving, we don't need to write anything more than the starting and ending squares. We use a dash to separate the starting and ending squares, and an "x" if the move was a capture.

SPECIAL NOTATIONS

Certain moves in chess have their own special notation:

• Castling king-side is denoted by "0-0"

• Castling queen-side is denoted by "0-0-0"

• When promoting a pawn, indicate the promoted piece in parentheses: for instance, "a7-a8(Q)" says that white moved a pawn to the a8 square and promoted it to a queen.

• Capturing en passant is denoted by "ep" after the move; for instance, "d5xc6 ep" shows a pawn capturing en passant on the c6 square.

We use exclamation points and question marks to comment on the ingenuity or effectiveness of moves. Here's what they mean:

ANNOTATION COMMENTS

! means a good move.
!! means a brilliant, completely unexpected move.
? means an error.
?? means a gross blunder, probably losing the game.

SECRETS OF THE ENDGAME

If you weren't able to checkmate your opponent in the middle game, or if you didn't win so much material that he decided to give up, you'll eventually reach an ending, and you'll need to know how to win it. That's the goal of this book – to show you the strategies that govern the ending, and teach you how to be a winning endgame player.

> **FIRST WORD**
>
> The endgame is the final phase of a chess game. Most of the pieces have been exchanged. The enemy kings remain, along with a few pawns, and at most one or two pieces on each side.

Endgames are different from openings and middle games – different principles, different priorities. Just because you play other parts of the game well doesn't mean you yet have what it takes to win in the endings. But after you've read this book, you will.

Is the endgame important? You bet it is! Look at it this way: in the endgame, you're trying to coordinate just one or two pieces, along with some pawns. If you can't master that, what hope do you have to coordinate a whole army of pieces and pawns in the middle game?

ENDGAME AND MIDDLE GAME DIFFERENCES

When you reach an endgame, many of the principles that governed the play in the middle game have to be set aside. New principles now govern the play, and you'll need to learn them. Here they are:

(1) The king is a fighting piece. In the opening and the middle game, your job is to keep your king safe from the attacks of the enemy queen, rooks, and minor pieces. Castling early is a good strategic idea – it gets the king to relative safety in the corner of the board, secure behind a rampart of pawns, while the center becomes a slugfest of two opposing armies.

In the endgame, that's all changed. Although the king is slow-moving, his ability to move in all directions makes him unstoppable once he starts vacuuming a nest of enemy pawns. Objectively, the king as an attacking piece is perhaps a little stronger than a single bishop or a single knight. In many endings, the first job is to get the king into the center.

(2) Pawns are important. In the middle game, pawns provide support for the pieces, and can be used as levers to break open enemy fortifications. But you must be careful – a pawn too far from its fellows is easily picked off. In the endings, a pawn's ability to become a queen makes it a powerful threat. Most endings revolve around the struggle to create a passed pawn, push it up the board, and turn it into a queen. The advantage of a single pawn, in the hands of an endgame master, is usually sufficient to win.

(3) Changing tactics. In the middle game, the players can employ the full range of tactical ideas that I outlined in my earlier book . Pins, forks, skewers, double attacks, and discovered checks all come into play.

In the endgame, with few, if any, pieces left, you won't see most of these tactics. Instead, a new kind of tactic surfaces: breakthrough combinations designed to get a pawn closer to the queening square. You'll see plenty of examples of these combinations in this book.

(4) Stalemate. When one side has to move, and isn't in check, but doesn't have a legal move, that's a stalemate, and the game is a draw. Stalemates just don't happen in the middle game. With plenty of pieces and pawns around, you can't run out of moves very easily. As both sides have less and less material, the possibility of a draw by stalemate looms larger. In some endings, a combination to induce a stalemate becomes the only way to salvage a draw in an otherwise lost game. I'll show you some examples along the way.

STRATEGY WITH ROOKS AND QUEENS

On the one hand, endgames with rooks and queens aren't all that different from other endgames. The king is still a fighting piece and needs to be mobilized, even though he'll be in a bit more danger with rooks or queen roaming around the board than he was facing weaker knights or bishops. Forcing a pawn through to queen is still the main idea, and queening combinations are often the key winning maneuver. Also, the defending side will still try to save himself with a creative stalemate trap when the opportunity arises.

However, there are a couple of strategic ideas that are unique to these major piece endings. Try to learn them, and notice how they're used in the endings that appear later in this book.

In rook endings, an active rook is usually the key to victory, often even more important than an extra pawn. You want your rook attacking key enemy pawns, forcing your opponent to use his valuable rook to defend his pawns. You also want your rook restricting the enemy king, confining him to the rear ranks or files along the edge of the board.

In endings with bishops or knights, the first strategic moves were usually spent centralizing the king. In rook endings, the top priority is maneuvering to activate your rook and to force your opponent into passivity. Only then do you bring the king into play. By following the examples in this book, you'll learn how to time and execute these maneuvers yourself.

With major pieces on the board, passed pawns are especially powerful. A queen plus a passed pawn is an irrepressible threat. Even an opposing queen can't stop their advance. A passed pawn supported by a rook behind it is almost as strong; your opponent can block the pawn with his rook, but at the cost of tying his rook down for the rest of the game.

In rook and queen endings, the play revolves around getting a passed pawn, pushing it as far as possible, then figuring out how to break through the defender's blockade. In this book, you'll learn all the secrets of these maneuvers.

THE LAYOUT OF THIS BOOK

I'll start in **chapter 4** by showing you how to execute all the basic checkmates. Once your last pawn is gone, you'll have to checkmate with just the pieces you have left. This chapter shows you how.

Chapter 5 covers endings with just kings and pawns. When all the pieces are gone, you'll have to know if you'll be able to force a pawn through to queen, or if your opponent can block you into a draw.

Chapter 6 shows endings in which each side has a knight in addition to kings and pawns, while **chapter 7** shows the same kinds of endings where both sides have a bishop.

Chapter 8 covers endings where one side's bishop battles the other side's knight. Each piece has characteristic advantages and disadvantages. Here you'll learn how to assess who holds the edge. In **chapter 9**, I'll show you how to stop an advanced pawn or two with your rook.

Chapter 10 covers the important endgame of rook and pawn against rook. I'll show you the basic positions that are draws, then the key maneuver that lets the stronger side force a win from a good position.

In **chapter 11**, we'll look at complex positions where rook battles rook with many pawns on the board. The key idea in these endings is an active rook position. I'll show you how to achieve an active position and make good use of it.

If a single pawn is far enough advanced, even a queen can have trouble stopping it. **Chapter 12** shows when the queen can win and when the pawn can draw.

Chapter 13 covers endings with queen and pawn against queen. In some cases, the queen and pawn can force a win. I'll show you how.

Endings with queens and many pawns are covered in **chapter 14**. An advanced passed pawn is a tremendous advantage in these endings, even more important than an extra pawn.

Chapter 15 looks at endings where a queen battles against two rooks. Usually these endings favor the rooks, especially if the board is wide-open. You'll learn how to take advantage of these special situations.

Let's get going!

BASIC CHECKMATES

How big an advantage do you need to force a checkmate with no extra pawns available to be promoted to queens? Here are the combinations of pieces that can force a checkmate against a lone king:

FIRST WORD

A basic checkmate means a situation in which the winning side (White in all of our examples) has only his king and one or two other pieces left against the enemy king. All the pawns have been exchanged off the board.

MATING COMBINATIONS

(1) king and queen

(2) king and rook

(3) king and two bishops

(4) king and bishop and knight

That's it. If, after all the pawns are gone, you don't have one of these advantages, you won't be able to force a checkmate. For example, if at the end of the game you have just a king and bishop against the enemy king – as in the following example – then you can't force a checkmate. (In fact, you can't even construct a position which is checkmate.) In this case, the players don't need to waste any time playing on. They can just shake hands and agree to a draw.

Diagram 2: King and Bishop vs. King

In the same way, king and knight against a lone king is a draw. Interestingly, so is king and two knights against a king! In this case, you can construct a position which is a checkmate, but you can't force it to happen. Black can always avoid the checkmate with a little alertness.

MATING WITH A QUEEN
We'll start with the most basic of all checkmates: White has a king and queen, and Black has just his king. Once you learn the right technique, it's a pretty easy checkmate to execute.

Usually this situation results after one side queens its last pawn. Take a look at Diagram 3, where White's on move.

Diagram 3: White on move

White's on move, and he has just one pawn left, on a5. Since it's his turn, he can just push the pawn up the board to a8 and make a queen. Black can't do anything to stop this plan, since his king, on f5, is too far away. After White makes a queen, however, he'll have to figure out how to force Black into a checkmate position. Let's watch and see how he manages this.

> **1   a5-a6**

The first job is to queen the pawn so White heads for a8 in a hurry.

> **1   ...   Kf5-e5**

What should Black do if he can't catch the pawn? The best idea is to maneuver the king into the center of the board. His king can't be checkmated unless he's actually on the edge of the board somewhere, so he should stay as far from the edges of the board for as long as possible. The center squares are a good place to start.

19

| 2 | a6-a7 | Ke5-d5 |
| 3 | a7-a8(Q) check | |

White makes a new queen and gives a check at the same time.

| 3 | ... | Kd5-e5 |

Black gets out of check and stays in the center at the same time.

Diagram 4: White on move

White has queened his pawn. Now what? Many beginners go astray at this point, by indulging in an orgy of mindless checks. For instance, a beginner might try 4 Qa8-e8 check Ke5-d5 5 Qe8-d7 check Kd5-e5 6 Qd7-b5 check Ke5-d4 7 Qb5-b4 check Kd4-d5. White's had some fun giving check, but he hasn't accomplished anything.

In fact, White can't achieve any progress until he brings his king into action. White has to force Black's king to the edge of the board, and he can do that only if his king and queen cooperate. Go back to the last diagram, and let's see how White should proceed.

4   **Kd1-d2!**

The right idea – the king swings into action.

4   ...   **Ke5-d4**

Black tries to stay in the center.

5   **Qa8-a5!**

The White queen cuts off the Black king from the whole top half of the board. Suddenly the king has only two legal moves, to c4 and e4.

5   ...   **Kd4-e4**

Black tries to stay as far away from an edge as possible.

6   **Qa5-c5!**

Now the left side of the board is off limits. Again, the Black king has only two legal moves, to f3 and f4.

6   ...   **Ke4-f4**

Black has been pushed out of the center squares.

7   **Qc5-d5**

White continues the process of herding the Black king to the edge. Notice that White has not given a single check. Instead, he uses his king and queen together to cut down on Black's available squares.

7   ...   **Kf4-g4**

Not much choice.

8   Kd2-e3

The White king and queen now control f3, f4, f5, g5, and h5. Black has only a few squares left.

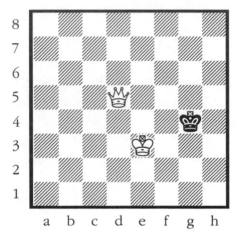

Diagram 5: Black on move

8   ...   Kg4-g3

Black tries to stay off the edge of the board.

9   Qd5-g5 check!

White's first check forces Black to an edge square.

9   ...   Kg3-h3

10   Ke3-f2

This forces checkmate next turn.

10	...	Kh3-h2
11	Qg5-g2 checkmate	

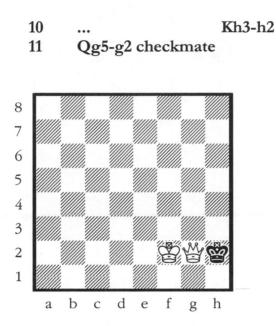

Diagram 6: Black has been checkmated

White could also have given checkmate by moving to the squares h4, h5, or h6.

Practice checkmating with the queen until you have the procedure down perfectly. From any starting position, you should be able to force checkmate in about ten moves.

MATING WITH A ROOK
Checkmating with an advantage of an entire queen isn't too difficult once you understand how it's done. However, you won't always be able to get an advantage that big at the end of a game. Sometimes your opponent is able to capture your last pawn when it queens.

Take a look at Diagram 7.

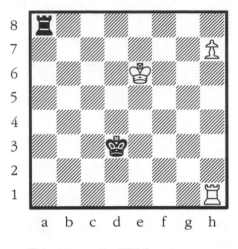

Diagram 7: White on move

White has an extra pawn, and it's about to queen. But Black's rook guards the queening square, so Black will be able to capture the new queen. After White recaptures, he will be left with just a single rook to force checkmate against Black's king.

There's nothing White can do to improve on this scenario. If White doesn't queen the pawn this turn, Black can force the issue by moving his rook to h8 and capturing the pawn on h7 next turn. So White has nothing better than to queen the pawn now, then figure out how to give checkmate with his single rook. Although it's a little more difficult than checkmating with a queen, it's still straightforward, as we shall see.

| 1 | h7-h8 (Q) | Ra8xh8 |

Black naturally gives up his rook for White's queen.

| 2 | Rh1xh8 | Kd3-d4 |

Once again, the best place for Black's king is in the center of the board. White can only checkmate Black by driving him to the edge of the board, so the longer Black stays in the center, the longer he can survive.

3   Rh8-h4 check

This check will drive Black into either the lower half of the board (if he plays K-e3, d3, or c3) or the upper-left corner (if he plays K-c5). Once Black is confined to one part of the board, White's job will be to shrink Black's area until he's finally pushed back to the edge.

3   ...   Kd4-c5

Diagram 8: White on move

Now what? At this point White needs to notice a crucial fact: If it were Black's turn to move, he would have to retreat and concede still more territory. In Diagram 8, Black's only legal moves are back to b5, b6, or c6, all squares which are closer to the edge of the board. Therefore White doesn't need to attempt anything dramatic – a do-nothing move will suffice.

4   Rh4-g4!

The right idea – White simply shifts his rook one square. Now it's Black's turn to move, and his king will have to retreat.

4   ...   Kc5-c6

Black would, of course, prefer not to move at all. But the rules say he must, so he tries to stay as far away from the edge of the board as possible.

5   Rg4-c4 check

When the kings are in opposition (facing each other with one square in between) a check with the rook enables White to make progress. Black's king can't remain on the c-file or d-file, so he is pushed back to the b-file, closer to the edge.

5   ...   Kc6-b5

The king retreats but attacks the White rook.

6   Ke6-d5

If White moved the rook, he would give up some of the ground he gained last turn. By defending the rook, he continues the process of herding Black's king to the side of the board.

6   ...   Kb5-b6

Diagram 9: White to move

Once again we've got a situation where White wishes it were Black's turn to move. If that were the case, White could either drive Black to the edge of the board or deeper into the corner. So White plays another waiting move.

7   Rc4-c1!

The rook retreats, and now it's Black's turn to move.

Notice something else in the position: the White rook doesn't need to be close to the enemy king. Since its power sweeps all the way across the board, it's just as effective from a distance. (Actually, it's even more effective, since the Black king can't threaten the rook when the rook is far away.) The same is true of the bishop and the queen, which are also long-range pieces, but not of the knight, which is a short-range piece.

7   ...   Kb6-b5

The only other choice was to move into the corner with Kb6-b7. That's no improvement.

> **8   Rc1-b1 check**

Once again, when the kings are in opposition, White makes progress with a rook check.

> **8   ...   Kb5-a5**

Black is finally forced to the edge of the board. It doesn't matter whether he plays to a4, a5, or a6, since White can quickly force checkmate in any case.

> **9   Kd5-c4!**

This sidestepping maneuver is actually the quickest way to win. Black has only two squares available to him: a4 and a6. But if he plays to a4, White will reply with Rb1-a1, checkmate. So Black has to head toward a8.

> **9   ...   Ka5-a6**
> **10   Kc4-c5!**

Once again, if Black moves forward with Ka6-a5, White has Rb1-a1 mate. So –

> **10   ...   Ka6-a7**
> **11   Kc5-c6   Ka7-a8**
> **12   Kc6-c7   Ka8-a7**

Once Black reaches the corner, no escape is possible. Then Black has to move forward.

> **13   Rb1-a1 checkmate**

Diagram 10: Black is checkmated

Checkmating with a rook should take 15-20 moves from the most unfavorable starting positions. Study this example carefully until you understand how to maneuver the enemy king to the edge of the board.

THE FIFTY MOVE RULE

Why is it important to be efficient in checkmating the enemy king? Because your opponent can eventually claim a draw if you don't seem to know how to execute a checkmate. It's called the fifty move rule, and it's usually stated as follows:

THE FIFTY MOVE RULE

If more than fifty moves elapse without a capture or a pawn move, either player has the right to claim a draw.

By the way, "fifty moves" refers to fifty moves on each side; that is, fifty moves by White and fifty moves by Black). The rule prevents games from continuing endlessly when the player with the advantage either can't win or doesn't know how to win. After fifty moves, his opponent can just claim a draw.

This rule isn't usually enforced in casual games, because players aren't keeping score, and without a written score, it's impossible to know when fifty moves have elapsed. But in tournament play, it's an important rule, so you should remember it.

MATING WITH THE TWO BISHOPS

Another checkmate that can arise over the board is two bishops and king against a lone king. Although two bishops are actually slightly stronger than a rook in the middle game, a checkmate with the two bishops is more difficult because the two pieces have to be coordinated properly. A strong player would have no difficulty with this ending, but many beginners might let the win slip away. Let's see how it's done.

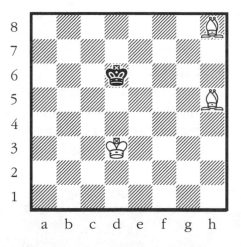

Diagram 11: White on move

As with the other endings, White is trying to activate his pieces, confine the enemy king to a small area, then push him back to the edge of the board.

1   Kd3-d4!

A good start. The king takes control of c5, d5, and e5, cutting off the lower half of the board.

1   ...   Kd6-e6

The Black king tries to scurry away. From e6, Black can move in two directions: back to d6 and e6, or forward to f5 and f4. The more avenues of movement Black has, the better his chance of escaping the trap.

2   Bh5-g4 check!

This cuts off one escape path. The White bishops now control f5 and f6, so Black either has to head back the way he came, or retreat toward the eighth rank.

2   ...   Ke6-d6

From d6, the Black king holds off the White king, while keeping as many escape routes open as possible.

3   Bh8-e5 check

The dark-squared bishop moves into play, cooperating with its partner to hem in the Black king.

3   ...   Kd6-c6
4   Bg4-f3 check

This pushes Black closer to the edge. His only available squares are now d7, b6, and b5.

4   ...   Kc6-b5

Black heads for the areas where White's pieces have less control. If White knows what he's doing, Black can't stop the checkmating process: he can only slow it down. But if White doesn't know what he's doing, Black may be able to prolong the process so much that he can claim a draw under the fifty move rule.

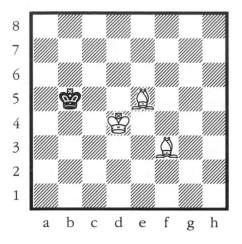

Diagram 12: White on move

5   Be5-c7!

By cutting off the squares b6 and a5, White is pushing the Black king down the board.

To administer a checkmate with two bishops, the Black king will actually have to be pushed into a corner, not just to the edge as with the queen and the rook. At some point, White needs to decide just what corner he's going to use. Here White has decided to checkmate Black in the a1 corner. (He could eventually maneuver Black into any corner, but with his king on d4, the a1 corner is most convenient.)

| 5 | ... | Kb5-b4 |
| 6 | Bf3-e2 | |

This move cuts off the b5 square. Now Black is confined to the lower left corner of the board.

| | 6 | ... | Kb4-b3 |

Black heads for a possible escape via c2 and d2.

| | 7 | Be2-d3 |

White cuts off c2.

| | 7 | ... | Kb3-b4 |
| | 8 | Bc7-d6 check |

Chases Black back toward the corner.

| | 8 | ... | Kb4-b3 |

Black tries to stay off the edge of the board.

| | 9 | Bd3-c4 check | Kb3-c2 |
| | 10 | Bd6-b4! |

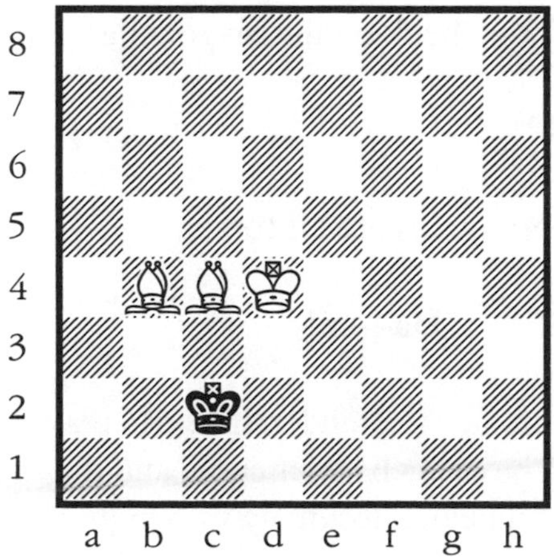

Diagram 13: Black on move

33

White's pieces cooperate very well. Black's king is now confined to the squares b2 and c2 and the edge squares a1-d1. If White's bishops remain where they are, the Black king can't escape from this box.

| 10 | ... | Kc2-b2 |
| 11 | Kd4-d3! | |

By taking away the c2 square, this pushes the king back to the first rank.

11	...	Kb2-c1
12	Bc4-b3	Kc1-b2
13	Bb3-a4	

Since the Black king will eventually be mated in the a1 corner, his box has to include the a1 square. By repositioning his bishop to a4, White lets the Black king reach the corner.

| 13 | ... | Kb2-a2 |
| 14 | Kd3-c2 | |

White doesn't want his king on the c3 square, since that would block a later bishop check on the diagonal a1-h8.

| 14 | ... | Ka2-a1 |

Black's remaining moves are all forced.

| 15 | Ba4-c6! |

White still has a chance to blunder. If he had played instead Ba4-b3, Black would have been stalemated, and the game would be a draw! Now White can checkmate in two more moves.

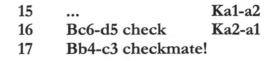

15	...	Ka1-a2
16	Bc6-d5 check	Ka2-a1
17	Bb4-c3 checkmate!	

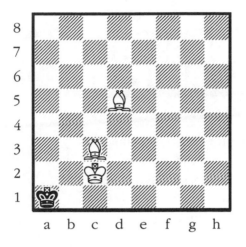

Diagram 14: Black has been checkmated

Play over this ending a few times and notice how well the bishops cooperate. By visualizing Black's possible escape routes, White was able to cut them off with his bishops and eventually pin Black's king in a corner. After that, the checkmate was pretty easy.

There's one more possible basic checkmate: king and knight and bishop against a lone king. It rarely occurs, so we won't give an example here. The proper approach is very similar to the checkmate with the two bishops.

ENDINGS WITH KINGS AND PAWNS

In the last chapter you learned how to checkmate the enemy king with a big material advantage. How do we get such an advantage? Usually by queening a pawn. In this chapter, you're going to see how to nurse an advantage of a pawn or two to victory.

FIRST WORD

What do you do if you're left with just your king and a few pawns in the endgame? In this chapter you'll learn how to win the game even with just these few pieces remaining.

KING AND PAWN AGAINST KING

The simplest way to win an ending of a king and pawn against a lone king is if the lone king isn't in position to stop the pawn. In this case, the pawn just marches up the board to victory. There's a simple way to tell if the enemy king can stop the pawn: take a look at what's called the square of the pawn.

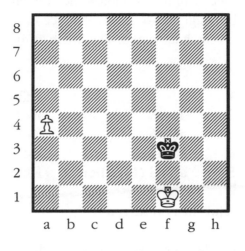

Diagram 15: Black on move

It's Black's move in Diagram 15. Can the Black king catch the White pawn? To find out, imagine a large square with the White pawn at one corner, extending up to the edge of the board. In Diagram 16, the square is indicated with 'x' marks.

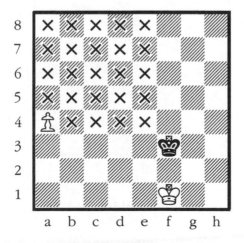

Diagram 16: The square of the pawn

If Black can move within this square, he can catch the pawn with his king. In Diagram 16, Black can accomplish this with Kf3-e4, so he can catch the pawn. The finish of the game might go as follows:

1	...	Kf3-e4
2	a4-a5	Ke4-d5
3	a5-a6	Kd5-c6
4	a6-a7	Kc6-b7
5	a7-a8 (Q) check	Kb7xa8

...and the game ends in a draw.

Can Black draw whenever his king gets within the square of the pawn? No. If White's king is in position to assist the pawn, sometimes White can push the pawn through to victory, sometimes not. Let's look at a few examples.

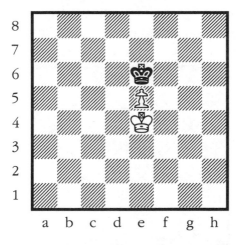

Diagram 17. Black to move

Here's a good position to remember: if White's king is behind his pawn, while Black's king is blocking the pawn, then Black will be able to draw with correct play. Watch how it's done.

38

1	...	Ke6-e7!

This is Black's basic idea. When he's forced to give way, he should always move his king straight back, not to one side.

2	Ke4-d5	Ke7-d7!

In this position Black is said to have the opposition. When the two kings oppose each other with one square in between, whoever does not have to move has the opposition. Having the opposition helps – it compels the opponent to give ground. In this position, White cannot force through with his king.

3	e5-e6 check

Since retreating the king would do no good, White has to advance his pawn.

3	...	Kd7-e7
4	Kd5-e5	Ke7-e8!

Again, Black retreats straight back. This will enable him to regain the opposition next turn.

5	Ke5-d6

If White goes to f6, Black can draw in the same way.

5	...	Ke8-d8

Black again has the opposition, and White must advance his pawn.

6	e6-e7 check	Kd8-e8

Now White has only one move to save his pawn...

| 7 | Kd6-e6 | Stalemate |

The Black king isn't in check, but he has no legal move. That's a stalemate, and the game ends in a draw.

If the White king can get in front of his pawn and gain the opposition, then he'll be able to push the Black king out of the way and queen his pawn. Take a look at Diagram 18.

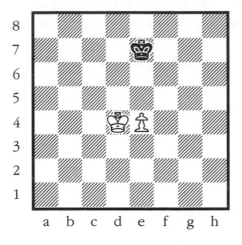

Diagram 18: White on move

If it were Black's turn to move, he could get a draw by playing 1... Ke7-d6! and we would have reached the previous example. If it's White's turn, he can win by playing as follows:

| 1 | Kd4-e5! |

With this move White gets the opposition. Now Black's king has to give way, and White can make more progress.

| 1 | ... | Ke7-d7 |

| 2 | Ke5-f6! | |

This is the winning idea, side-stepping the enemy king.

| 2 | ... | Kd7-e8 |
| 3 | Kf6-e6! | |

Once again White gets the opposition and Black has to give way.

| 3 | ... | Ke8-f8 |
| 4 | Ke6-d7! | |

With this last sideways step, the White king now controls the queening square (e8). Once White's king can control this square, the pawn can march straight through and Black can't stop it.

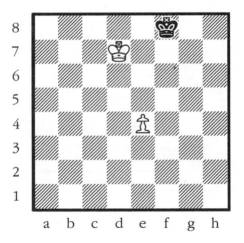

Diagram 19: Black on move

4	...	Kf8-f7
5	e4-e5	Kf7-f8
6	e5-c6	Kf8-g7
7	e6-e7	Kg7-f7
8	e7-e8 (Q) check	

41

That's it. With his extra queen, White forces checkmate according to the example in the last chapter.

The basic winning idea is to use your king to push the enemy king out of the way. If you can get in front of your pawn and get the opposition, your opponent can't stop you from executing this plan.

DRAWING ON THE ROOK FILE

If White's pawn is on either of the rook files (the a-file or h-file), then this maneuver won't work and the game is a draw even if White can get in front of his pawn with the opposition. Take a look at Diagram 20:

Diagram 20: White to move

White can get the opposition, but look what happens.

| 1 | Kb5-a6 | Ka8-b8 |

White should now move to his left to execute the side-stepping maneuver, but he's out of space! He has to move back to his right, and the Black king ends up stalemated in the corner.

42

2	a4-a5	Kb8-a8
3	Ka6-b6	Ka8-b8
4	a5-a6	Kb8-a8
5	a6-a7	Stalemate

The rule to remember is as follows:

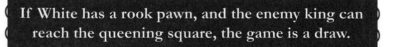

If White has a rook pawn, and the enemy king can reach the queening square, the game is a draw.

KING AND TWO PAWNS AGAINST KING

An advantage of two pawns is very big – these endings tend to be easy wins. Diagram 21 shows a typical situation.

Diagram 21: White on move

If Black tries to capture one pawn, the other will have time to run through to queen.

1	f4-f5	Kc6-d5
2	b4-b5	Kd5-e5
3	b5-b6	Ke5xf5
4	b6-b7	

White gets a queen next turn.

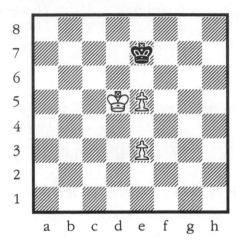

Diagram 22: White on move

If White's pawns are doubled (both on the same file), he can win by using the second pawn to gain a move when necessary. In Diagram 22, White's king can't get in front of the pawn. Normally this means the game is a draw, but here the extra pawn lets White win.

| 1 | e5-e6 | Ke7-e8 |

Moving straight back is the right idea for Black, as you learned before.

| 2 | Kd5-d6 | Ke8-d8 |

Black takes the opposition.

| 3 | e6-e7 check | Kd8-e8 |

Diagram 23: White on move

If White didn't have the pawn on e3, he would now have to play Kd6-e6, stalemating Black. But because he has the extra pawn, he can force Black's king out from his blocking position.

> **4   e3-e4!**

White gains a move. Now it's Black's turn, and he has to move, even though he doesn't want to.

> **4   ...   Ke8-f7**
> **5   Kd6-d7!**

Now White controls the queening square. Next turn he plays e7-e8 (Q), and wins easily.

PAWNS ON EACH SIDE

When both sides have pawns, the basic winning idea is:

- Try to get a passed pawn on one side of the board.
- Push that pawn toward the queening square, forcing Black to move his king to stop it.
- Using that pawn as a decoy, bring your king to the undefended side of the board and win the pawn there.

The decoy technique is crucial to most of the more complicated king and pawn endings. Let's look at a couple of examples.

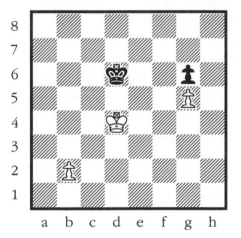

Diagram 24: White on move

In Diagram 24, White has two pawns, Black only one. The b-pawn is White's passed pawn (no enemy pawns blocking its path to the queening square), so it looks like the more dangerous of the two. But it's really the g-pawn that's eventually going to be a queen. The b-pawn is just a decoy.

	1	b2-b4		Kd6-c6

46

If Black ignores the b-pawn, White will be happy to push it through. So Black moves over to capture it.

> **2   Kd4-e5!**

The White king heads for his real objective – the Black pawn on g6.

2	...	Kc6-b5
3	Ke5-f6	Kb5xb4
4	Kf6xg6	Kb4-c5

Black heads to the other side, but he can't get there in time.

5	Kg6-f7	Kc5-d6
6	g5-g6	

White will queen his pawn on g8.

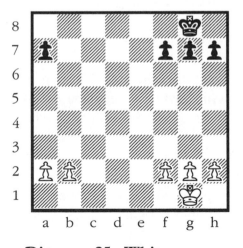

Diagram 25: White on move

In Diagram 25, White has five pawns, and Black has only four. White's extra pawn gives him a potentially winning advantage

47

if he plays well. The key to the ending is White's advantage of two pawns versus one on the queen's side of the board (the a-, b-, and c-files). This will eventually allow White to create an outside passed pawn, a pawn that's far away from the bulk of pawns back on the king-side.

The winning strategy in this ending consists of five steps:

1. Centralize the king.
2. Advance the queen-side pawns to create a passed pawn.
3. Use that pawn as a decoy to deflect Black's king.
4. Invade the undefended king-side with the king.
5. Capture enough pawns to ensure victory.

Let's see how White carries out the plan.

1	Kg1-f1

The first job is to centralize the king. The king is a slow-moving piece, and it takes him awhile to get to the scene of the action. If you centralize him first, he'll be ready to go where he's needed.

1	...	Kg8-f8

The same advice applies to Black. In the absence of any direct threat, Black should put his king in the center, ready to move to either side.

2	Kf1-e2	Kf8-e7
3	Ke2-d3	Ke7-d6
4	Kd3-d4	

Phase I accomplished. The king is optimally placed in the center, ready to move to either side.

4	...	f7-f6

Black can't make any progress with his king, so he waits for White to try something.

Why didn't Black try something more aggressive, like f7-f5? The answer is this: when you're on the defensive, you're generally better off leaving your pawns alone. The farther you advance your pawns, the easier it is for White to attack them. (This should make sense, since you're moving the pawns closer to White's king.) Leaving the pawns far back makes White's job as hard as possible.

5	b2-b4!

Phase 2 starts. White advances his a- and b-pawns to make a passed pawn on the queenside.

5	...	a7-a6

Stops the White pawn from advancing any farther.

6	a2-a4

This will threaten to play b4-b5 next turn.

6	...	Kd6-c6

This stops b4-b5 for the time being.

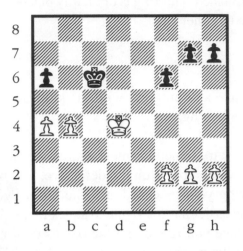

Diagram 26: White on move

7	f2-f4

White starts to advance his king-side pawns. This will have the effect of pinning Black's pawns in place, making them easier to capture when White's king moves into position.

7	...	g7-g6
8	g2-g4	

Although Black should be reluctant about moving his pawns, White doesn't need to be so cautious. White doesn't have to worry about Black's king invading his pawns since the Black king can never move far from the White pawn on the b-file.

8	...	h7-h6
9	Kd4-c4	

White's king will now help push the pawn to b5.

9	...	g6-g5

Black doesn't have many choices. His king is already on the best possible square, so rather than move it, he advances the king-side pawns again.

10	f4-f5!

A GOOD RULE OF THUMB FOR MOST ENDINGS

When you're losing, try to exchange pawns; when you're winning, try to keep as many pawns as possible on the board. If the defender can exchange all the pawns, he can usually draw. The more pawns he can exchange, the closer he gets to that goal. For the side who's winning, of course, the opposite holds true.

So White avoids exchanging and instead pushes forward.

10	...	Kc6-d6

Black has run out of good moves, so he tries to keep White's king out of d5. From d5, White could threaten to push into e6.

11	b4-b5!	a6xb5 check
12	a4xb5	

Phase 2 accomplished. White has a passed pawn on the queen-side, just three moves from the queening square. Black must try to stop it.

12	...	Kd6-c7

Phase 3 accomplished. The Black king has been decoyed from guarding the entrance route to the king-side. Next step: invasion!

| 13 | Kc4-d5! | Kc7-b6 |

Black has to pick off the b-pawn at some point.

| 14 | Kd5-e6! |

Invasion accomplished. The Black pawns fall like ripe fruit.

14	...	Kb6xb5
15	Ke6xf6	Kb5-c6
16	Kf6-e7	

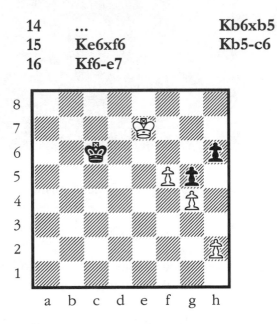

Diagram 27: White's f-pawn will queen

White could capture the other pawns, but it's not necessary. The quickest way to win is to advance the f-pawn to f8, making a queen. Black's king can't stop the pawn. White should win easily.

Study the winning procedure in this ending carefully, since the basic idea – create a passed pawn, decoy the enemy king, and invade with your own king – is fundamental to most king and pawn endings.

TACTICAL TRICKS

Not all king and pawn endings require grand strategy. Sometimes a quick tactical stroke can decide the game – if you see it! Here's some examples of the kind of ideas to look for. When you find them, they can win an apparently drawn (or even lost) game.

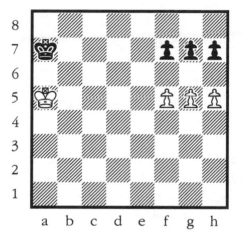

Diagram 28: White on move

At first glance, this game looks like it might peter out to a draw. The pawns are even, and White's king can't force its way through. If White tries Ka5-b5, Black keeps the opposition with Ka7-b7. After Kb5-c5, Black plays Kb7-c7, and so forth. So how can White win?

Amazing as it seems, White can queen a pawn on the king side without any help from his king! Here's how he does it:

$$1 \qquad g5\text{-}g6!$$

This looks like it will just lead to an exchange of pawns.

1	...	h7xg6
2	f5-f6!!	

What's this? White seems to be giving up a couple of pawns.

2	...	g7xf6

Black has to capture or White will play f6xg7, queening the pawn.

3	h5-h6!

...and wins! In two turns, the pawn will push through to h7 and h8, queening. After that, it will be easy to pick off Black's pawns and deliver checkmate.

Could Black have saved himself with a different capture on the first turn? The answer is no. If Black had played (after 1 g5-g6) f7xg6, White would have won in a similar way:
2 h5-h6! g7xh6 3 f5-f6 and queens.

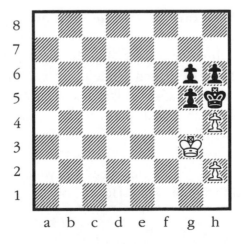

Diagram 29: White on move

In Diagram 29, it looks like White might have to struggle to draw, with Black having an extra pawn on the kingside. Actually, White can force checkmate in just four moves! Here's how he does it:

1	h2-h3!

Exchanging pawns (with h4xg5) might lead to a draw, but White has an amazing idea.

1	...	g5xh4 check

Now Black is two pawns ahead, and thinking about winning the game himself. What could go wrong?

2	Kg3-f4

Suddenly Black finds himself a little short of moves. Fortunately, he still has one, and it's a check.

2	...	g6-g5 check
3	Kf4-f5	

Black realizes that his two extra pawns are just boxing in his king. He still only has one move, and this time it's not even a check.

3	...	g5-g4
4	h3xg4 checkmate!	

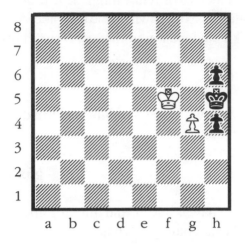

Diagram 30: Black is checkmated

White's last pawn was enough to administer checkmate.

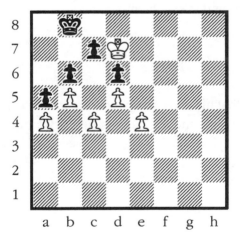

Diagram 31: White on move

In Diagram 31, White has an extra pawn, but Black seems to have established a solid defensive position. This position illustrates a key rule in king and pawn endings: getting a new queen is so important that any number of pawns can be sacrificed to achieve it. In this position, White can actually break through Black's apparently solid structure by sacrificing some pawns to clear the way for one pawn which will eventually queen.

1   c4-c5!!

White starts the breakthrough process. This move induces a weakness somewhere in Black's position.

1   ...   b6xc5

This is the only way to capture. If Black tries the other capture, d6xc5, White's e-pawn marches straight through to queen on e8.

2   b5-b6!

The purpose of this sacrifice is to deflect the pawn that guards the d6 square.

2   ...   c7xb6

Again, no choice. White was threatening to play b6xc7.

3   e4-e5!

One more sacrifice, this time to clear the way for the pawn on d5.

3   ...   d6xe5
4   Kd7-e7

The king gets out of the way for the pawn to advance.

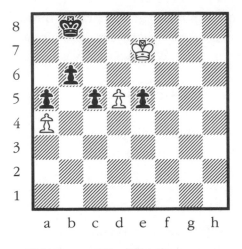

Diagram 32: Black on move

Black is now two pawns ahead, and in fact two of his pawns have clear roads to their queening squares (c1 and e1). Unfortunately, White will queen first, and with check, after which his powerful queen will easily stop the Black pawns.

| | 4 | ... | e5-e4 |

Pushing the c-pawn instead leads to the same result.

	5	d5-d6	e4-e3
	6	d6-d7	e3-e2
	7	d7-d8 (Q) check	

queening with check buys White the one vital tempo he needs to catch Black's pawn.

| | 7 | ... | Kb8-b7 |
| | 8 | Qd8-d2! | |

58

That's it. White will capture the e-pawn next turn, after which his king and queen will be able to force checkmate.

SAVING THE DRAW

Chess isn't only about winning. Turning an apparent loss into a draw with a clever maneuver can be just as important. Let's look at a couple of examples of how ingenious defensive play can save a half-point.

Diagram 33: White on move

Even though White is on move in Diagram 33, his position looks hopeless. Even if he got to make two moves in a row, he's too far behind to catch Black's pawn on the h-file. And his own pawn on c6 can be easily stopped by Black's king. (If he plays c6-c7, Black replies Ka6-b7 and takes the pawn next turn.)

Nonetheless, White has a way to save the draw. The key is to combine two operations at once: chasing Black's pawn and saving his own. If each one of his moves can perform double duty, he can just squeeze out a draw. Watch.

1	Kh8-g7!	

Moving along the diagonal is the key to White's maneuver. He simultaneously moves one step closer to Black's pawn and one step closer to his own.

1	...	h5-h4

Black's king is still in position to stop White's pawn, so he confidently moves his own pawn to queen.

2	Kg7-f6!	

Once again, moving along the diagonal brings White both one step closer to Black's pawn and one step closer to his own.

2	...	Ka6-b6

Since Black's pawn is still out of range of White's king, Black moves over to capture the pesky pawn.

3	Kf6-e5!	

The third double purpose move in a row saves the game for White. If Black captures White's pawn, White can play Ke5-f4 and pick off the Black pawn. So Black has to try to queen.

3	...	h4-h3
4	Ke5-d6!	

The White king arrives just in time.

4	...	h3-h2
5	c6-c7	Kb6-b7
6	Kd6-d7	h2-h1 (Q)

7	c7-c8 (Q) check	

With queen against queen, the result is a draw.

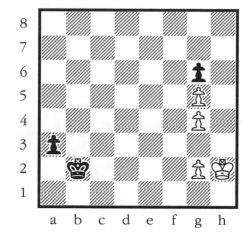

Diagram 34: White to move

Although White is two pawns ahead in Diagram 34, his game looks utterly hopeless. Black's pawn queens so quickly that White can't possibly advance his own pawns in time. For instance, after 1 h3-h4 a3-a2 2 h4-h5 a2-a1 (Q) 3 h5xg6 Kc3-d3, Black's new queen stops the pawns from advancing and Black will pick them off after Qa1-g7 next turn.

However, White has a way to save the game.

1	Kh2-g3	a3-a2
2	Kg3-h4	

Where's he going?

2	...	a2-a1 (Q)
3	g2-g3!	

White shuts the door and prepares for a little nap.

No matter what Black plays, White has stalemated himself! An ingenious save.

6

KINGS, KNIGHTS, AND PAWNS

The knight and the bishop are called the "minor pieces," as opposed to the rook and queen, which are the "major pieces." Knowing the proper way to use these pieces is crucial to good endgame play. Let's start by comparing the bishop and the knight.

BISHOPS & KNIGHTS: MERITS & DEMERITS

The bishop is a long-range piece. It can zip all the way across the board in a single move. Unfortunately, since it moves along diagonals, it's always confined to squares of just one color.

If you still possess both your original bishops, this weakness isn't very noticeable. Two bishops working together can cover all the squares on the board. If you have only a single bishop, however, you may have problems. If your opponent has his pawns on squares of the opposite color from your bishop, you won't be able to attack them. If *your* pawns are on the same color squares as your bishop, they may get in the bishop's way.

What about the knight? Compared to the bishop, the knight is a short-range piece. It hops just a couple of squares each turn.

Because of its peculiar move, however, the knight changes the color of the square it lands on each turn. That fact provides the knight with its critical strength: it can eventually attack all the squares on the board.

If your opponent has just a bishop, and you put your pawns on the opposite-colored squares from the bishop, your opponent can't attack them. But that's not true with the knight. No matter where your pawns are, your opponent's knight can eventually attack them. That means you must be very alert in endings with just knights on the board. You'll have to make sure that your opponent's knight doesn't snap up your pawns, while staying very alert for chances to gobble his pawns.

HOW TO HANDLE THE KNIGHTS

Let's take a look at a typical ending where both sides have a knight left.

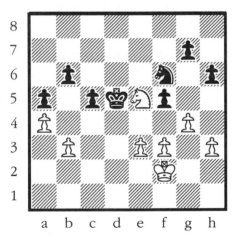

Diagram 35: White on move

This endgame is from a game between former World Champion Anatoly Karpov and Grandmaster Artur Yusopov, from the tournament at Dortmund in 1997. It's White's move, and right now the material is even, with both sides having a knight and six pawns. Black even has one advantage, in that his king is already centralized at d5, while White's king is stuck back at f2.

White, however, has some advantages of his own. His knight is actively placed in the center of the board, at e5. But his most important advantage is Black's weak pawns. The pawn at b6 is fixed in place (it can't move forward without being captured), and it supports the other two Black pawns at a5 and c5. If the pawn on b6 goes, Black's whole queenside could eventually disappear.

Now, White appears to have some weak pawns, too. The pawn at b3 is undefended, as is the pawn at h3. Does this somehow compensate for Black's weak pawn at b6?

The answer is no, and the reason is crucial to an understanding of how to play endings well. *A weakness isn't really a weakness unless you can attack it.* White's pawns on b3 and h3 could be weaknesses, if Black could get at them with his knight, but he can't. The Black knight (on f6) just isn't in position to reach those squares. But the White knight can move to c4, which attacks the pawn on b6. That means Black's weakness is a serious problem.

Let's see how a former World Champion handles this endgame.

1   Ne5-c4!

White's knight was attacked, so he moves it to safety, while beginning the attack on the pawn at b6. Now White has two threats: Nc4xb6 and g4xf5. Black can't defend both pawns at once, but he seems to have an adequate defense.

1   ...   f5xg4

This capture looks like it will solve the problem. White will recapture on g4, Black thinks, and then he will have time to defend the b6-pawn with his king by playing Kd5-c6. But White sees a little farther into the position...

2   Nc4xb6 check!

One of the secrets of winning endgame play is accurate calculation. The player who can see a move or two farther than his opponent has a big advantage when the number of pieces is small and a lot hinges on every move.

What White has seen is that after Black gets out of check by attacking the knight with 2 ... Kd5-c6, White will just play back, 3 Nb6-c4. Then if Black captures another pawn with 3 ... g4xh3, White can play 4 Kf2-g3, regaining the h-pawn. Eventually, White will capture both the pawns on h3 and a5, and he'll be a pawn ahead. Winning a pawn is the first step to winning the endgame.

Can Black do anything to counter this plan? Not really. Black can't get his king or his knight around to guard the a5 pawn, and he won't be able to reach the pawn on h3 either. He'll have to try to save the game at a later point.

A pawn ahead doesn't guarantee victory in a minor piece ending. The problem is that if the defender (Black in this position) can exchange enough pawns, he may be able to give up his knight if he can exchange it for White's last pawn or pawns. White would be left with an extra knight, but if he loses all his pawns in the process, he won't be able to deliver checkmate. (Remember the lesson from an earlier chapter: a single knight or a single bishop against a lone king can't force a checkmate.)

As the defender, Black's strategy will be to force the exchange of pawns whenever he can. If he can reduce White to a single pawn, he can sacrifice his knight for that pawn and draw.

White's strategy will be to make as much progress as he can while keeping several pawns on the board. As in the endings with just kings, White would like to get a passed pawn and use it as a decoy, so he can win more pawns elsewhere on the board.

Back to our game.

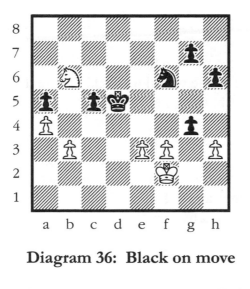

Diagram 36: Black on move

2	...	Kd5-c6

Black has no better square for the king.

3	Nb6-c4

White hops back and now attacks the pawn on a5.

With the knight guarding the b6 square and White's a4-pawn guarding the b5 square, the Black king can only guard the pawn on a5 by moving to b7 and a6. But as soon as the king gets to b7, White can play Nc4xa5 with check, so Black can't save the pawn.

> ## ENDGAME KNIGHT PLACEMENT
> The best placement for a knight in endgames with blocked pawns is on a square of the same color as its own pawns. It then attacks squares of a different color than the pawns, which yields maximum control over the board.

3	...	g4xf3

At first glance the move g4xh3 might look stronger. However, after that move White would play Kf2-g3 and then Kg3xh3, so White will be capturing the Black pawn in any event.

Black's actual capture is best since it leaves White with two disconnected, isolated pawns (on e3 and h3) rather than two connected pawns (on e3 and f3). Connected pawns have the ability to advance and defend each other, while isolated pawns have to be defended by pieces.

4	Kf2xf3

After White captures the pawn on a5, which can't be saved, he will have four pawns against Black's three, giving him a significant advantage. The real weakness in Black's position, however, is the fact that his knight can't get into position to attack any weak spots in White's game. If Black plays Nf6-h5, he still can't get to the squares g3 and f4. If he plays Nf6-d5, he can get to the squares b4 and c3, but he still can't attack anything.

White has an active knight since it cooperates with its own pawns and attacks weak pawns in Black's position. Black has a passive knight, since he can't do any of those things.

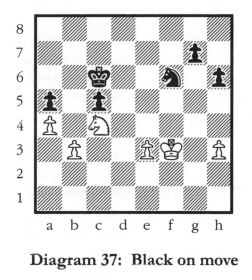

Diagram 37: Black on move

4   ...   Kc6-d5

There's no way Black can save his pawn on a5, so he's not going to waste any time on it. Instead, he centralizes his king again. By attacking the e4 square, the Black king and knight prevent the passed e-pawn from advancing.

5   Nc4xa5

Although the pawn can't be saved, White still needs to take it right away, so that his knight can then be redeployed for other duties.

White's next job will be to get the knight back into the center (probably via the c4 square), then concentrate on advancing his two passed pawns, the a-pawn and the e-pawn.

5	...	g7-g5

The g5-square is a good one for a Black pawn. With the Black knight on f6 controlling e4 and g4, and the pawn controlling f4 and h4, the White king is shut out of the game for awhile. In addition, Black may be able to get a passed pawn of his own, by playing h6-h5 and g5-g4.

What's the potential value of a passed pawn for Black? Basically, it will serve as a decoy. If White has to chase down a Black passed pawn, Black may have time to gobble up one or two of White's pawns. Remember that to draw this game, Black is going to have to eliminate the four White pawns. Exchanges work in Black's favor. If Black can somehow trade his three pawns for three of White's pawns, then sacrifice his knight for White's last pawn, he'll get his draw. That's his goal, and we'll see how close he can come to achieving it.

6	Na5-c4

White brings his knight closer to the action and clears a path for his a-pawn to start marching. He must be a bit careful; the pawn is securely protected where it is, but as it moves up the board, it gets farther from White's pieces and closer to Black's.

6	...	h6-h5

Black has decided to push forward and make his passed pawn, while exchanging off a pair of pawns in the process. He doesn't really have any other plan to try. If either his knight or his king move, White can advance his passed e-pawn.

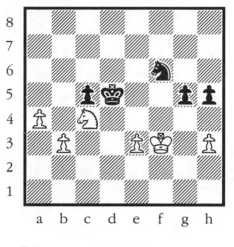

Diagram 38: White on move

7   Nc4-d2!

White retreats to advance. He wants to start pushing his e-pawn, so he brings another piece to bear on the e4-square. He's imagining a sequence like 8 e3-e4 check Kd5-e5 9 Nd2-c4 check Ke5-e6 10 e4-e5! moving deep into Black's territory and paving the way for his king to advance to e4.

7   ...   Kd5-e5

Black can't stop the pawn from advancing, so he gets out of the way of the check.

8   e3-e4

The pawn begins to move. Now White threatens 9 Kf3-e3 and 10 Nd2-c4 check, pushing Black back.

8   ...   Nf6-e8

Black can't stop White's plan, so he starts to regroup. The knight isn't doing anything on f6, and if the Black king has the job of stopping the e-pawn, someone is needed to stop the a-pawn. So Black starts to reposition his knight. The knight is headed for c7, a6, and b4. From the b4-square it can keep an eye on the center while stopping the a-pawn from reaching a6.

Moving the knight prevents Black from pushing his pawn to g4, getting a passed pawn. But the two Black pawns are keeping White's king out of that area of the board, and Black may get a chance to push them later.

9   Kf3-e3

On e3 the White king keeps Black out of d4. Now White is ready to play Nd2-c4 check or even Nd2-f3 check.

9   ...   Ne8-c7

Black heads for a6 and b4.

10   Nd2-c4 check

White gains more territory.

10   ...   Ke5-f6

It's good technique not to get in the way of your own pieces. By retreating to f6 (instead of e6) Black keeps the e6-square open for his knight. The knight may not go there (Black's main plan is still to relocate it to a6 and b4) but there's no harm in preserving the option, especially since Black's king is just as active on f6 as e6.

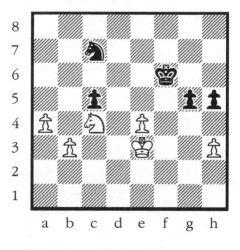

Diagram 39: White on move

How should White make progress from this position? Right now his pawn on e4 and his knight on c4 control the squares d5, e5, f5, keeping Black's king and knight confined to passive positions. If White pushes right ahead with 11 e4-e5 check, however, the Black king takes up residence on f5, and then it would be Black, by controlling the squares f4, e4, and d4, who would be keeping White out of the center!

White decides to maintain his position in the center for a couple of turns, while turning his attention to the king-side. If he can exchange some of the pawns on the g and h-files, he might be able to create a new route for infiltration.

> **11   Ke3-f2**

Heading for g3.

> **11   ...   Nc7-a6**

Black's knight will continue to block the a-pawn, while Black awaits developments on the king-side.

| 12 | Kf2-g3 | Na6-b4 |

Both sides take up their positions.

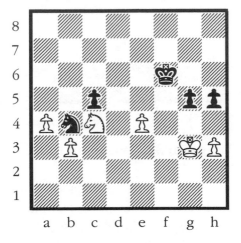

Diagram 40: White on move

| 13 | h3-h4! |

White makes his move, breaking up Black's pair of pawns on the king-side. Whether Black captures or pushes past with g5-g4, White will attain his objective: access to the f4 square for his pieces.

This kind of thinking is characteristic of endgame play. Unlike the middle game, where players look for combinations to win pawns or pieces, in the endgame players strive to make slow but steady progress, battling for the control of individual squares. It's like the contrast between hand-to-hand combat and mechanized warfare. On this level, access to a single key square can be the difference between a win and a draw.

13	...	Nb4-c6

If Black starts the exchange of pawns with g5xh4 check, White's king advances as he recaptures. If Black waits for White to exchange with h4xg5 check, his own king will advance with Kf6xg5. Whoever captures first thus loses ground, a good endgame tip to remember.

From c6, the knight guards the e5 square. Now after 14 h4xg5 check Kf6xg5 15 e4-e5? Kg5-f5! Black wins the e-pawn.

14	a4-a5!

White opens another front. Now his passed pawn threatens to move to a6, which will tie Black's knight to guarding the a7 square.

14	...	Nc6-b4

The only move to stop the pawn from advancing while keeping the knight reasonably active.

15	Nc4-d2!

With Black's knight now tied down, White's next job is to resolve the situation on the king-side in his favor. By moving to d2, White prepares to play Nd2-f3, which will force the pawn on g5 to move. Then the f4 square will open for White's king to push forward.

15	...	Nb4-c6

Black is running out of moves. If his king goes to e5, White wins after h4xg5, with a two-pawn advantage. Now the knight threatens to take the pawn on a5.

16	a5-a6

White avoids capture my moving closer to the queening square. Now Black's knight really is riveted in place.

16	...	g5xh4 check

Black will be forced to make this capture after White plays Nd2-f3, so he plays it now, while White's knight is still a bit out of play back on d2.

17	Kg3xh4

Now the White king takes aim at the weak pawn on h5.

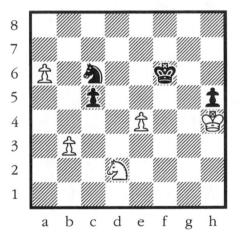

Diagram 41: Black to move

17	...	Kf6-e6

Black could have saved his h-pawn by playing 17 ... Kf6-g6. Why didn't he?

Black probably saw that with his king all the way over on the king-side, White would be able to win the c-pawn in the following sequence: 17 ... Kf6-g6 18 Nd2-c4 Kg6-h6 19 Nc4-a5!! Nc6-a7 (if Black captured White's knight, White would play a6-a7 and queen next turn) 20 Na5-b7!, followed by 21 Nb7xc5. The combination of the e-pawn, b-pawn, and a-pawn would win for White very quickly.

Instead Black tries for his last chance. He's going to let White capture the h-pawn (incidentally leaving White's king away from the scene of the action), then use his own king to capture White's advanced a-pawn, while his knight sacrifices itself for White's e-pawn. If he can then manage to trade his c-pawn for White's b-pawn, he'll have his draw.

Can White defeat that plan? Let's see.

18	Kh4xh5

First things first. White has to eliminate the passed h-pawn, then plan to get his king back to the center in time.

18	...	Ke6-d7

There's no way for Black to capture the a-pawn except with his king. That's a problem with knights in the endgame.

KNIGHTS AND PASSED PAWNS
If a pawn is *mobile* (able to advance), then a single knight can never force its capture. If the knight attacks the pawn, the pawn can simply advance. To capture a passed pawn, the knight has to control the pawn while the king hunts it down.

To get to the pawn, the Black king will have to follow the route d7-c7-b8-a7-a6. When the Black king gets to c7, the White knight will go to c4, preventing Black from taking the quicker route via b6.

19   Kh5-g6

The White king moves to support the passed e-pawn. Black will have to deal with this pawn with his knight.

19   ...   Kd7-c7

Black will move to b6 next turn (if White allows it).

20   Nd2-c4!

White controls the b6-square, forcing the Black king to take the long march via b8 and a7.

20   ...   Kc7-b8

The White pawn can't be saved, but Black will use a lot of time capturing it.

21   Kg6-f6

The White king is now ready to help push his e-pawn up the board. Eventually, Black will have to give up his knight for this pawn.

21   ...   Kb8-a7

Closing in on the a-pawn.

22   e4-e5

The White pawn heads up the board. Black doesn't have to capture it until it reaches e7.

22	...	Ka7xa6
23	e5-e6	Ka6-b5
24	e6-e7	Nc6xe7

Black waited as long as possible; he must capture the pawn.

25	Kf6xe7

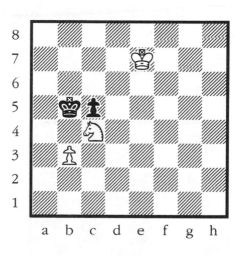

Diagram 42: Black on move

White has won Black's knight, but the game isn't over yet. When Black's king gets to b4 and attacks the last White pawn, White will have to move his knight back to d2 to defend it. Black will be able to capture the knight on that square, but can he then get back and capture White's last pawn in time? Karpov has done his calculation and decided that Black will be one move short. Let's watch the finish.

25	...	Kb5-b4
26	Nc4-d2	

The only way to hold onto the pawn.

26	...	Kb4-c3
27	Ke7-d6!	

If White loses his last pawn, his winning chances go with it. So he has to let the knight go, but it costs Black one too many moves to take the knight.

27	...	Kc3xd2
28	Kd6xc5	Kd2-c3
29	b3-b4!	

The pawn finally comes under the king's protection and heads for b8. Black can't stop it, so he gives up.

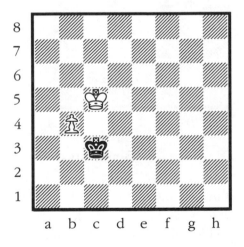

Diagram 43: Black can't stop the last pawn

White's winning plan in this endgame was very instructive. Most endings in which each side has a knight will follow a similar course. White's plan breaks down into six steps:

> **ENDGAMES WITH OPPOSING KNIGHTS**
> 1. Win a pawn. (This usually happens before the end-game is reached.)
> 2. Move the king and knight to the best available positions.
> 3. Advance pawns to create a passed pawn.
> 4. If necessary, exchange pawns to create an avenue into the enemy position.
> 5. Advance a passed pawn and win the enemy knight.
> 6. Use your own knight to win the last enemy pawns.

In this ending, we saw Karpov employ all six steps of the plan.

KNIGHT VERSUS PAWN

Many knight and pawn endings resolves into a struggle of a lone knight against the opponent's last pawn and king. Sometimes the knight can stop the last pawn, and sometimes he can't. Let's look at a couple of examples.

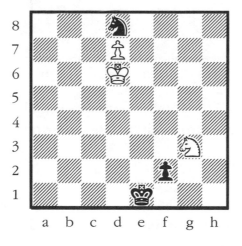

Diagram 44: Black on move

Black can win White's knight for his pawn on f2, but then what?

| 1 | ... | f2-f1 (Q) |
| 2 | Ng3xf1 | Ke1xf1 |

Now White has just his last pawn against Black's lone knight. With just a knight left, Black can't win. But what about White?

The answer is no. As long as Black's knight can reach the circuit of squares b7, d8, and f7, he can prevent the pawn from advancing. Take a look at the next diagram.

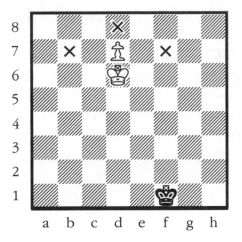

Diagram 45: The drawing squares for Black's knight If he can stay on this circuit, he can draw the game.

3	Kd6-e7	Nd8-b7
4	Ke7-e6	Nb7-c5 check!
5	Ke6-d6	Nc5xd7
6	Kd6xd7	Draw

There was no way White could have chased the Black knight away from guarding the d8 queening square.

The knight does a good job against center pawns, since it can move to either side of the pawn as need be. A rook pawn is considerably more dangerous. Take a look at the next diagram.

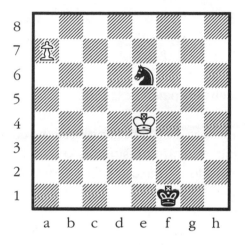

Diagram 46: Black on move.
White will be able to force a queen.

Although Black's knight can reach the queening square, he doesn't have much to do once he gets there!

| 1 | ... | Ne6-c7 |

Stops the pawn for the moment.

| 2 | Ke4-e5 | Nc7-a8 |

Anywhere else, and the pawn just queens.

| 3 | Ke5-d6 | Kf1-e2 |
| 4 | Kd6-c6! | |

A knight in the corner only has two available squares. Now White guards both of them.

83

4	...	Ke2-d3

If the knight moves, White just takes it.

5	Kc6-b7	Kd3-c4
6	Kb7xa8	Kc4-c5
7	Ka8-b7	

...and White queens his pawn next turn.

Had Black's king been a little better placed, he could still have drawn this ending, even after losing his knight. In Diagram 46, move Black's king to g3 instead of f1. Now, he has a clever drawing maneuver.

1	...	Ne6-c7
2	Ke4-e5	Nc7-a8
3	Ke5-d6	Kg3-f4
4	Kd6-c6	Kf4-e5

So far the same as before, but Black's king is moving in a little faster. Still, the king won't get there in time to save the knight.

5	Kc6-b7	Ke5-d6
6	Kb7xa8	Kd6-c7

And White is stalemated! The game ends in a draw.

If White has a rook pawn but it's advanced only as far as the sixth rank (it was on the seventh in the last two positions), Black can stop it with his knight if the knight can reach the circuit of squares a7-c8-d6-b5, as marked in the next diagram.

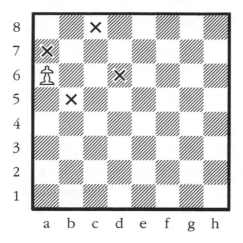

Diagram 47: Black can draw if his knight can reach the circuit marked with an 'x'.

Once Black is on this circuit, he can either block the pawn's advance or capture it with a knight fork. Here's an example:

Diagram 48: White on move

It's White's turn, but Black's knight has reached one of the key blocking squares. White tries to chase the knight away.

1	Kc5-b6	Na7-c8 check
2	Kb6-b7	Nc8-d6 check
3	Kb7-b8	Nd6-b5

White's not making much progress. He can move the knight around, but it always ends up blocking the pawn's advance from one of the key squares. White has one more try:

4	Kb8-b7	Kf1-e2
5	Kb7-b6	Nb5-d6
6	a6-a7	

Has White broken through?

6	...	Nd6-c8 check!

No! This knight fork saves the day.

7	Kb6-b7	Nc8xa7

And Black gets a draw.

Once you know the secret of the circuit, some apparently lost endings can be cleverly saved. Take a look at the next one.

Diagram 49: White on move

Black's king is too far away to stop the pawn, so the job is up to the knight. He can save the draw, if he can find the right road to the circuit.

1	a2-a4	Ng5-f3!

The right path isn't necessarily the shortest one. Black has a couple of checks at his disposal, but both lead to dead ends.

If Black tries the obvious 1 ... Ng5-e4 check, White replies with 2 Kd6-c6, controlling b5 and d6, two of the key squares on the circuit. The only unguarded square is then c8, which Black has to reach via e7 and g8, but that takes too long to arrange: 2 ... Ne4-f6 3 a4-a5 Nf6-g8 4 a5-a6 Ng8-e7 check 5 Kc6-b7! and White's pawn slips through. A similar situation results if Black starts with 1 ... Ng5-f7 check because White plays 2 Kd6-c7!

2	Kd6-d5!

White's best winning try, attempting to block out the knight. If White plays 2 a4-a5, Black actually stops the pawn easily with 2 ... Nf3-d4! threatening to get on the circuit with 3 ... Nd4-b5. White can stop that only by playing 3 Kd6-c5, but then Black plays Nd4-b3 check and Nb3xa5.

By the way, remember this relationship between the king and the knight (king two squares away from the knight along a diagonal). It's the best position for the king to be in to prevent the knight from moving toward the king. In fact, it takes the knight three turns just to give check from this position!

	2	...	Nf3-h4!

Incredibly, Black has used two valuable moves to get his knight one square *further* away from the pawn as it was in the beginning. Now, however, he's on the right path to reach one of the key squares.

	3	a4-a5	Nh4-f5!

This is the key square for the knight. He now has two possible routes to the circuit: Nf5-e7-c8 and Nf5-d4-b5. If White just pushes the pawn with 4 a5-a6, Black gains a move with check: 4 ... Nf5-e7 check 5 Kd5-c5 Ne7-c8 and Black has stopped the pawn.

	4	Kd5-c6	Nf5-d4 check!

Now Black threatens to play Nd4-b5, stopping the pawn.

	5	Kc6-b6	Nd4-f5!

Once again, Black makes progress by reversing direction.

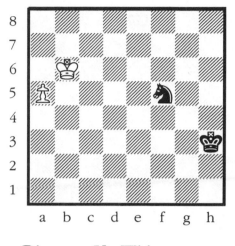

Diagram 50: White on move

6   a5-a6

If White tries to keep the knight out of d6 by playing 6 Kb6-c7, Black has 6 ... Nf5-d4! (heading for b5) 7 a5-a6 Nd4-b5 check and Black gets on the circuit and draws.

6   ...   Nf5-d6

Black has reached the circuit. Next turn the knight plays to b5 or c8, depending on White's move.

TACTICS WITH THE KNIGHT

The knight's ability to leap around obstacles and fork the opponent's pieces makes it a dangerous piece in tight situations. Be especially alert to the knight's possibilities, no matter which side of the board you're on. The knight can generate winning possibilities out of seemingly hopelessly drawn positions. We'll wind up this chapter with three examples of the knight's surprising power. Would you believe that any of these three positions could be won by White?

89

Diagram 51: White to move

How can White possibly win this game? He has just one pawn left, and it's firmly under control by both Black's pawn and knight. In addition, Black's king is within the square of the pawn and much closer than White's. So what's the trick?

| 1 | Nd6xb7 check! |

White starts with a knight fork! If Black doesn't capture, White just plays Nb7xc5 with an easy win.

| 1 | ... | Nc5xb7 |
| 2 | a5-a6! | |

The idea is not to recapture the knight, but just to sneak through to the queening square. Suddenly Black's pieces are tripping over each other. If Black moves the knight, say Nb7-d6, White just plays a6-a7 and queens next turn.

| 2 | ... | Kd8-c7 |

> 3   a6-a7!

The lowly pawn takes control of b8 and can't be stopped. A good example of the awkwardness of the knight around the edge of the board.

Diagram 52: White to move

Black seems to have built an impenetrable little nest for himself in the corner. If White brings his king closer, by Kd7-c7, Black is stalemated. If White captures Black's last pawn with his knight, Black recaptures and picks off the pawn next turn, also with a draw. If White does nothing, Black just shuttles his king from a8 to b8. Can White make any progress, or is the game just a draw?

Actually, the game is far from a draw. In fact, White announces checkmate in five moves! Here's how.

> 1   Na5-c6!

The knight stalemates the Black king in the corner, so Black has only one move: capture the knight.

91

1	...	b7xc6
2	Kd7-c7	

Now it's clear: White has eliminated the stalemate by allowing Black's pawn to move.

2	...	c6-c5
3	b6-b7 check	Ka8-a7
4	b7-b8 (Q) check	Ka7-a6
5	Qb8-b6 checkmate!	

When the knight gives itself up so that a pawn may advance decisively, as above, it is called a *"clearance sacrifice."*

Diagram 53: White on move

One last example of the knight's strange powers. Black would have a draw if his last pawn wasn't on the board. Because he has an extra pawn, he loses!

1	Nc5-e4	Kh1-h2

If Black advances his pawn, h3-h2, White has Ne4-g3 check-mate.

2	Ne4-d2

The knight comes around the back way. Ne4-g3?? stalemates Black.

2	...	Kh2-h1
3	Nd2-f1	h3-h2

Now the king can't move, so the pawn advance is forced.

4	Nf1-g3 checkmate!

7

KINGS, BISHOPS, AND PAWNS

Unlike the knight, which takes slow, stuttering steps, the bishop sweeps around the board on the diagonals. It can move from one side of the board to another in a single swoop. This long-range power means that the bishop doesn't have nearly as much trouble stopping far-away pawns

FIRST WORD

The bishop is a very different piece from the knight. Its long range of motion makes it very useful for attacking far-away pieces.

as the knight did. Take a look at Position 54:

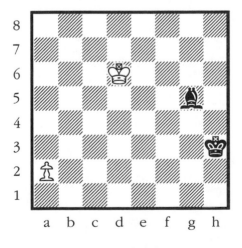

Diagram 54: White on move

This is Diagram 49, with a Black bishop on g5 instead of a Black knight. As we saw in the previous chapter, the knight on g5 can stop the pawn from queening, but it takes foresight and a very clever maneuver to pull it off. The knight had to start with the route Ng5-f3-h4!-f5 before it could be sure to reach the critical squares.

A bishop, however, stops the pawn without breaking a sweat.

1	a2-a4	Bg5-d2!

That's it. The bishop shuttles back and forth along the e1-a5 diagonal until White gets bored and pushes the pawn, then Black captures it on a5 with a draw.

Is the bishop just a better piece than the knight? It's not quite that simple. The bishop has one big drawback: it can only move to half the squares on the board. That means that a dark-squared bishop, like the one in Diagram 54, can't ever guard any of the light squares. Under the right circumstance, particularly with all the pawns on one side of the board, the bishop can be weaker than the knight.

In general, in most endings, the bishop's long range makes it a bit stronger than the short-hopping knight. But it's a small edge on average.

SAME-COLOR & OPPOSITE-COLOR BISHOPS

When both sides have one bishop left, there's a key feature of the position that has to be considered. Do the bishops travel on the same color squares, or not? If they do, they're called *same-color bishops*. If not, they're called *bishops of opposite color.*

For the most part, it's much harder to win an ending with opposite-colored bishops. The reason is that your opponent has total control over half the squares on the board, enabling him to set up barriers that can't be crossed. Take a look at Diagram 55:

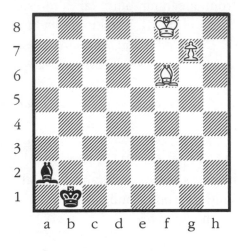

Diagram 55: White on move

White is ahead by a pawn, and it's a passed pawn on the seventh rank, ready to queen. Black's king and bishop couldn't be farther from the action, yet Black has no worries. He simply keeps his bishop on the a2-g8 diagonal, and whenever White plays g7-g8 (Q), he captures the new queen with his bishop, drawing the game. White has no way to cut off the bishop's guard of g8.

With same-colored bishops, it's quite a different story. Take a look at Diagram 56.

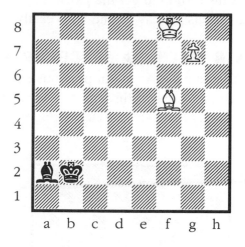

Diagram 56: White on move

Now the win couldn't be simpler.

1	Bf5-g6	Kb2-c3
2	Bg6-f7!	Black gives up

By interfering with the Black bishop's guard over g8, White queens the pawn next turn.

Incidentally, White had another way to win in Diagram 56. It takes a couple of moves longer, but the maneuver will play a big role in some other endgames, so let's take a look at it:

1	Bf5-h7	Kb2-c3
2	Bh7-g8	

White pushes the Black bishop onto a different diagonal.

2	...	Ba2-b1
3	Bg8-f7	Bb1-h7
4	Bf7-g6!	

97

White sacrifices his bishop to get the pawn through. After 4 ... Bh7xg6, White queens his pawns and wins easily.

HOW TO WIN WITH SAME COLOR BISHOPS

Take a look at Diagram 57. As in our previous example, White can eventually force his pawn through to queen. But he's got to be a bit more clever here, since Black's king is now close on the scene.

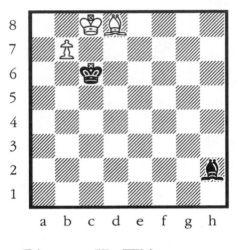

Diagram 57: White on move

White's goal is to oppose bishops on the h2-b8 diagonal, forcing Black to either trade bishops (after which the pawn queens) or move his bishop away (same result). Here his problem is to get his own bishop on the diagonal in the first place. With Black's king at c6, White can't play Bd8-c7 any longer, since Black would just take the bishop off. The only way to get his bishop on the crucial diagonal is to get to a7 and then b8. What's the best route to a7? Let's see.

1   Bd8-h4!

The right idea. White plans to move Bh4-f2, Bf2-a7, and Ba7-

b8, forcing Black's bishop off the diagonal. If Black allows this maneuver, he'll lose just as in our previous example. For instance, move White's bishop to b8 in this position, and the last few moves would be 1 ... Bh2-g1 2 Bb8-h4 Bg1-a7 3 Bh4-f2! and Black's bishop can't hold the pawn anymore.

What's Black to do? He has to try to stop the White bishop from getting to a7. Since his own bishop is pinned down to guarding b8, he'd better use his king.

1	...	Kc6-b6

Looks okay so far. When he gets to a6, he'll stop the bishop from moving to a7.

2	Bh4-f2 check	Kb6-a6

Mission accomplished. The bishop can't go to a7, and Black's bishop is still holding the pawn. Now what?

3	Bf2-c5!

This is what's known in the trade as a "waiting move." Black's king can't go anywhere without allowing the bishop into a7. Black's bishop can't leave the long diagonal, so he has to move to another square along the diagonal, either g3, f4, or e5. It actually doesn't matter which of those squares he picks – White will have the same winning idea in either case.

3	...	Bh2-g3

Now White can win, since he's shoehorned the bishop out of the cozy h2 square. Watch and see what a difference that makes.

4	Bc5-e7

Threatening to play B-d8 and B-c7, winning by opposing bishops.

4	...	Ka6-b6

Black has to move back to c6 to stop that plan.

5	Be7-d8 check	Kb6-c6

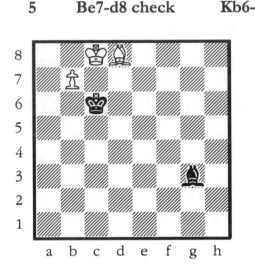

Diagram 58: White on move

Compare Diagram 58 to Diagram 57: what's changed? Only the
position of Black's bishop, which has been nudged from h2 to
g3. Why is that significant?

6	Bd8-h4!!

Because of this shot! White gets to simultaneously move the
bishop toward the g2-a7 diagonal while gaining a move by attacking the bishop. When Black's bishop was on h2, it couldn't
be attacked from this direction!

6	...	Bg3-h2

100

If Black takes the bishop, the pawn just queens. But the move it takes Black to save his bishop prevents him from getting his king to b6.

7	Bh4-f2	Bh2-f4
8	Bf2-a7	Bf4-g3
9	Ba7-b8	

Now White wins just like in the previous example.

9	...	Bg3-f2
10	Bb8-f4	Bf2-a7
11	Bf4-e3!	

Now the Black bishop has to give up covering b8. Black surrenders.

Not all these positions with an extra pawn are winning for White. In these last two examples, Black was hampered by the fact that, of the two diagonals leading to the queening square (or the next square that the pawn has to cross). One was long (h2-b8, 7 squares long) but the other was short (a7-b8, only two squares long). Once Black's bishop gets caught on the short diagonal, he's in trouble.

If both diagonals leading to the key square are fairly long, the defender is probably all right. Take a look at the next position.

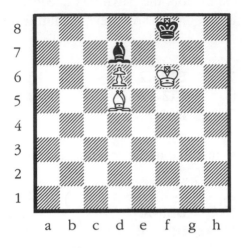

Diagram 59: White on move. Black can draw with good play

In Diagram 59 White has a center pawn, which gives Black better chances to draw since the two diagonals leading to the key square d7 are both long enough. (a4 to e8 is 5 squares while h3 to c8 is 6 squares). Those long diagonals mean that Black's bishop has plenty of maneuvering room. He still has to be alert, but here's how play might proceed.

1	Bd5-f7	

White's first job is to stop the Black king from getting in front of the pawn. If the king reaches d8, it can never be dislodged, and Black just moves around forever with his bishop.

1	...	Bd7-a4

Black keeps an eye on d7 from one of the diagonals.

2	Bf7-g6	Ba4-d7
3	Bg6-h5	Bd7-h3

Now the Black king is cut off from d8; White controls e8, e7, and f7. At this point White has to get his king to a square where he controls both the advancing square (d7) and the queening square (d8) and which isn't the same color as Black's bishop. There are only two such squares: e7 and c7. He's not going to reach e7, since Black's king on f8 keeps him out. So the only winning try involves heading for c7. Here he goes.

4	Kf6-e5	Kf8-g7

The Black king shadows the White king. When White reaches c7, Black needs to be attacking the pawn from e5.

5	Ke5-d5	Bh3-d7

Forces the king to take the long way around.

6	Kd5-c5	Kg7-f6
7	Kc5-b6	Kf6-e5
8	Kb6-c7	

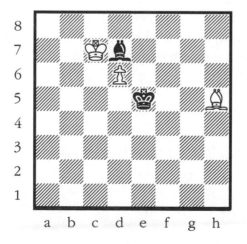

Diagram 60: Black to move

The White king is in position, now attacking the Black bishop. Black can guard the bishop with his king, or move it along either diagonal. Only one of these plans will save the game, while the other two will lose. Do you see the right idea?

8	...	Bd7-f5!

This is it! The other two plays would lose. If Black guarded with his king, Ke5-e6?, White would win with the skewer attack, Bh5-g4 check! and Bg4xd7. (If you didn't see this idea, you might want to review the chapter on skewers in the book , the third book in the "Road to Chess Mastery" series.)

How about the other try, guarding d7 along the shorter diagonal, 8 ... Bd7-a4? In that case, White would push his pawn through by playing 9 Bh5-f3! and 10 Bf3-c6!, blocking off the Black bishop. Only Black's actual move (or the equivalent Bd7-h3) holds the draw. The key idea is that Black must attack the d7 square along the diagonal where White's king doesn't control a blocking square. The two blocking squares are c6 and e6. White's king controls c6. Therefore Black wants to keep attacking d7 along the diagonal leading through e6. This forces White, if he wants to oppose bishops, to get his bishop to d7. But on that square, it actually blocks the pawn, giving Black a spare move to reposition the bishop.

9	Bh5-e8

White's only idea is to push the Black bishop off this diagonal.

9	...	Ke5-d5
10	Be8-d7	Bf5-c2!

Black is forced off, but he's ready to come back along the other diagonal.

11	Bd7-g4	Bc2-a4
12	Bg4-f3 check	Kd5-c5

Now that the Black king also guards c6, the Black bishop can safely stop the pawn from the shorter diagonal. White can't make any progress, so he agrees to a draw.

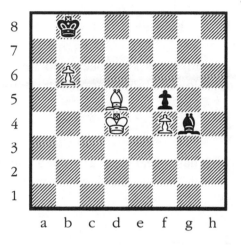

Diagram 61: White on move

Diagram 61 shows a more complicated endgame. White has two pawns this time, Black only one. White has a passed pawn, but he can't possibly queen it since Black's king is unassailably located on the queening square, and White can't ever dislodge it. That means that any winning try for White has to involve capturing Black's last pawn and then trying to queen his f-pawn, using the advanced b-pawn as a decoy.

So White will try to implement this plan. What's his first step?

White has the luxury in Diagram 61 of deciding just where he wants his pieces before he tries anything decisive. Notice that White's two pawns are on dark squares, so Black's bishop can't attack them. And White controls the squares a7, b7, and c7 with his bishop and pawn, so Black's king is confined to the last rank. That means that White should be able to position his king and bishop to their ideal squares before he goes after Black's pawn. That's a good rule to remember in endgames.

White decides to put his king on e5 and capture the pawn.

1	Kd4-e5	Kb8-c8

Black decides to shuffle his king back and forth until White moves his bishop, allowing him to approach the b-pawn.

2	Bd5-g2!	

A nice move, which has a neat tactical point a couple of moves down the road. White freezes Black's bishop at g4. Why that matters will soon become clear.

2	...	Kc8-b8
3	Ke5-f6	

The king heads for g5, where it attacks the Black bishop.

3	...	Kb8-c8
4	Kf6-g5	Kc8-b8

106

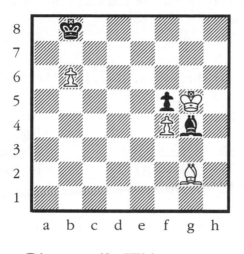

Diagram 62: White on move

5   Bg2-e4!

Now you see why White wanted Black's bishop to stay on g4. If Black captures the White bishop with 5 ... f5xe4, White replies with 6 Kg5xg4, and the ending with just pawns on the board is an easy win. White's king stops the Black pawn on e4. Black's king has time to stop either one of the White pawns, but it can't stop them both. A typical finish would be 6 ... e4-e3 7 Kg4-f3 e3-e2 8 Kf3xe2 Kb8-b7 9 f4-f5 Kb7xb6 10 f5-f6, and Black can't get inside the square of the f-pawn.

5   ...   Bg4-h3

Black's only chance is to keep the bishops on the board.

6   Be4xf5   Bh3-g2
7   Bf5-h7!

Prevents Black from stopping his pawn from the e4-square. If Black tries to stop the pawn on the other diagonal, with 7 ...

Bg2-h3, White plays 8 Bh7-e4 and keeps his b-pawn also.

| 7 | ... | Kb8-b7 |

If Black can't play B-h3 or e4, this is his only reasonable try.

8	f4-f5	Kb7xb6
9	f5-f6	Bg2-d5
10	Kg5-g6	Kb6-c7
11	Kg6-g7	Kc7-d7
12	Bh7-g8	

And Black has to give way and let the pawn through.

HOW TO WIN WITH OPPOSITE COLOR BISHOPS

As I mentioned before, endings where one side has a bishop travelling on the light squares while the other side has a bishop moving on dark squares – bishops of opposite colors – are much more likely to be drawn than endings with bishops of the same color. The defending side has a much better chance of establishing an impenetrable blockade. Look at Diagram 63:

Diagram 63: White to move

White is two pawns ahead, the pawns are connected and passed, and White's pieces seem to be in fine positions – but it's all for naught. Black's blockade can't be broken. His king sits forever on b6, and he just shuttles his bishop between g1 and c5. White can't ever push his pawn to c5 without losing it, so he has to agree to a draw.

But not all endings with bishops of opposite colors are drawn. Sometimes an advantage of a pawn or two can be pushed through to victory, provide the defender cannot set up a blockade such as we just saw.

Let's take a look at a few examples.

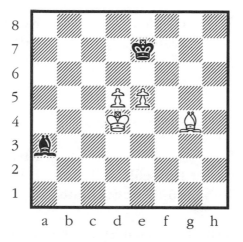

Diagram 64: White on move

In Diagram 64, White has kept his pawns abreast, which is good strategy. In that way, the pawns can threaten to advance at the proper time. Right now, it's too soon for either pawn to advance. If White plays 1 e5-e6?, Black plays Ba3-d6 with a permanent blockade. If White plays 1 d5-d6 check?, Black just sacrifices his bishop for the two pawns with 1 ... Ba3xd6 2 e5xd6 check Ke7xd6, draw.

First White needs to prepare the way by repositioning his king:

1   Kd4-c4!

The idea is to come around to c6, to help the pawns advance. If Black now attacks the pawn on dark with 1 ... Ba3-b2, White just plays 2 d5-d6 check Ke7-e8 3 Kc4-d5, and White's pawns are pushing through.

1   ...   Ke7-e8

Black doesn't want to go back, but he doesn't have a lot of moves.

2	d5-d6	Ke8-d8
3	Kc4-d5	Kd8-e8
4	e5-e6	Ba3-b4
5	e6-e7	

The d-pawn shields the e-pawn from capture by the Black bishop.

5	...	Bb4-d2
6	Kd5-e6!	Bd2-g5
7	d6-d7 checkmate	

A small change in the position of Black's bishop can make a big difference in these endings. Take a look at Diagram 65.

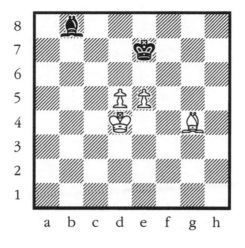

Diagram 65: White on move

In Diagram 65, the position is just the same as in Diagram 64, except we've moved Black's bishop from a3 to b8. This small change is enough to turn the position from a win for White into a draw! Why? Now Black's bishop not only guards d6 against the pawn's advance, it also attacks the pawn on e5. If White advances this pawn to e6, Black sets up a blockade as before with Bb8-d6. But if White doesn't advance this pawn, his king has to stay in the area d4-e4-f4-f5, so he never has time to get the king to c6, and his d-pawn can never advance.

Drawn game.

If White is two pawns ahead, but the pawns are disconnected, then White would like the pawns to be as far apart as possible. If the pawns are two files apart or more, there are many winning chances. The next page shows an example.

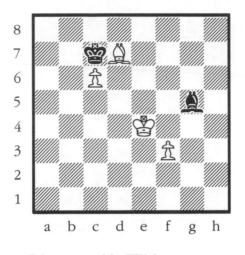

Diagram 66: White on move

In Diagram 66, White's pawns are two files apart. Black's king stops one pawn, while his bishop stops the other. White's idea is to use his king to push the pawn that the bishop is blocking. If he can win the bishop for that pawn, he'll be able to queen the other pawn eventually.

1	f3-f4	Bg5-f6
2	Ke4-d5	Bf6-c3

Black can't directly stop the pawn for awhile, since his king has to stay near the c-pawn. The crucial part of the ending doesn't happen until the pawn gets close to the queening square. Meanwhile, Black shuffles around, while forcing White to work a little.

3	Kd5-e6	Kc7-d8
4	f4-f5	Bc3-d4
5	f5-f6	Bd4-c3

Now White's king will move to the other side of the f-pawn, trying to escort it home.

6	Ke6-f5	Bc3-d4
7	Kf5-g6	Bd4-c5
8	f6-f7	

If White plays instead 8 Kg6-g7, Black could slow him down by pinning the pawn with 8 ... Bc5-d4. Then White would have to move the king back.

8	..	Bc5-f8

Blocks the pawn and stops White from playing his king to g7.

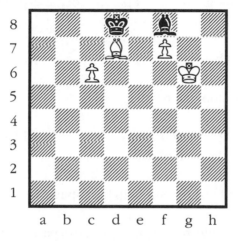

Diagram 67: White on move

9	Kg6-h7

It's important, when studying endgames, to think about how a small change in the position might affect the outcome. Noticing key features of a position will make you a much better player in the long run!

Notice, for instance, that if we moved the entire position one file to the right (so that White's pawns started out on the d-file and g-file) this outflanking maneuver wouldn't be possible, since White would be blocked by the edge of the board. In that case, the position might be a draw!

9	...	Kd8-e7

The king has to help guard f8.

10	Kh7-g8	Bf8-h6
11	Bd7-e8	

The f-pawn now guards the bishop, so the c-pawn is free to advance.

11	...	Ke7-d8

Black can only stop one of the pawns.

12	f7-f8 (Q)	Bh6xf8
13	Kg8xf8	

White's king and bishop will help the c-pawn through to queen.

When both sides have pawns, a single extra pawn is not necessarily a winning advantage. The defending side will have plenty of counterchances, and will often be able to fight his way to a draw.

The following are good rules for the defender to know.

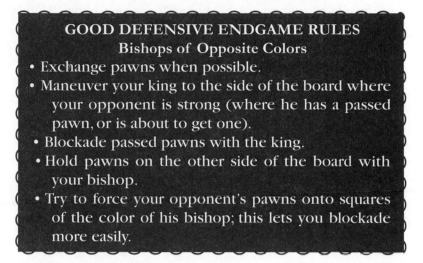

GOOD DEFENSIVE ENDGAME RULES
Bishops of Opposite Colors
- Exchange pawns when possible.
- Maneuver your king to the side of the board where your opponent is strong (where he has a passed pawn, or is about to get one).
- Blockade passed pawns with the king.
- Hold pawns on the other side of the board with your bishop.
- Try to force your opponent's pawns onto squares of the color of his bishop; this lets you blockade more easily.

Of course, the side trying to win wants to prevent all these things from happening. Let's look at a few examples to see how these games actually play out.

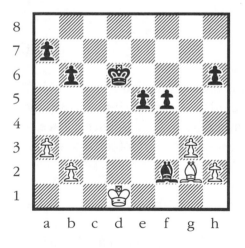

Diagram 68: White on move

White's a pawn down in Diagram 68, and he'll have to fight for a draw. His problems right now are on the king-side, where Black has an extra pawn. He'll need to make sure his king goes to that area. Black has a passed pawn already. On the e-file,

White needs to make sure his king blocks that pawn. Here's how he proceeds:

1   Bg2-h3

White starts by attacking the only pawn left on the white squares. If he can exchange that pawn, his task will be easier; fewer pawns favor the defender.

1   ...   Kd6-e6

Black's not interested in exchanging pawns just yet, so he guards f5 with his king.

2   Kd1-e2

White moves his king up to blockade. He also sets a subtle trap. Will Black fall in?

2   ...   Bf2-d4!

Black avoids the trap. White had apparently left a pawn for the taking. Black could have won the h-pawn by playing 2 ... Bf2-g1. But here's what would have happened: 3 Ke2-f1 Bg1xh2?? 4 Kf1-g2, and the bishop gets smothered to death. Endgames are full of such little traps. Watch out!

3   b2-b3   Ke6-f6

Black is trying to find a route into White's position with his king. He'll maneuver the king to g5, then perhaps play something like h6-h5-h4, looking to break through.

4   g3-g4!

116

A nice move, trying to put the Black pawns on dark squares. If White can then control the White squares, he'll have an adequate blockade.

4	...	Bd4-g1

If Black tries 4 ... f5-f4, White blockades everything with the moves Bh3-g2!, Ke2-d3, and h2-h3. Black has to keep the position flexible, so he goes after the h-pawn, which will make his own h-pawn a passed pawn. Now the bishop can't be trapped in the corner, because White has moved his g-pawn.

5	g4xf5	Bg1xh2
6	Ke2-f3	Bh2-g1
7	Kf3-e4	

White uses his king to block one of the passed pawns, while guarding his own pawn at the same time. Now the bishop is free to block the h-pawn.

7	...	Bg1-c5
8	a3-a4	

With the pawns on white squares, Black can never attack them. The draw is getting closer. The only question now is whether or not Black can advance his h-pawn.

8	...	Bc5-f8

Black is planning to guard the e-pawn from the rear, so that his bishop can simultaneously stop White's pawn from advancing to f6.

9	Bh3-f1

White starts marking time until Black makes his move.

9	...	Bf8-g7
10	Bf1-e2	Kf6-g5
11	Be2-d3	h6-h5
12	Bd3-f1	

White will blockade the pawn on the h3 square.

12	...	h5-h4

This basically concedes the draw, but Black can't do better. If he tries to move his king in ahead of the pawn, White can drive it back. After 12 ... Kg5-g4, White plays Bf1-e2 check, and Black either has to retreat or block the pawn with his king.

13	Bf1-h3	Kg5-f6
14	Bh3-g4	

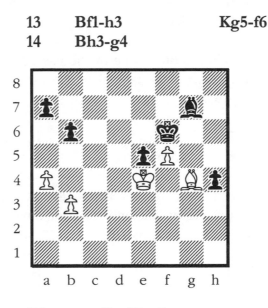

Diagram 69: Black on move

White's blockade is now secure. Black agreed to a draw.

An advantage of two pawns is generally enough to win, even with bishops of opposite colors. The process can be long, but the ideas are similar to those we've seen before:

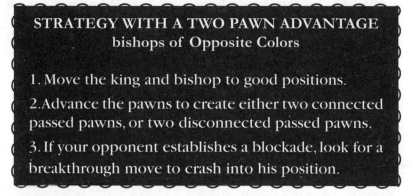

STRATEGY WITH A TWO PAWN ADVANTAGE
bishops of Opposite Colors

1. Move the king and bishop to good positions.

2. Advance the pawns to create either two connected passed pawns, or two disconnected passed pawns.

3. If your opponent establishes a blockade, look for a breakthrough move to crash into his position.

In the next position, White shows how it's done in practice.

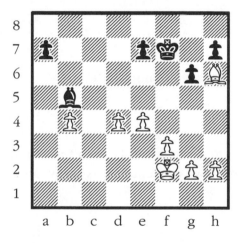

Diagram 70: White on move

White is two pawns ahead, but he doesn't have a passed pawn anywhere yet. He must create one on the king-side or in the center, where he has an advantage of five pawns against three.

1   Bh6-f4

As in most endings, the first job is to move the pieces to good squares. The bishop is out of play on h6, so White puts it on a better diagonal.

1   ...   Kf7-f6

Black, meanwhile, just waits for White to start something.

2   Bf4-b8

The idea here isn't to capture the a-pawn (presumably Black will realize that it's attacked and move it) but to get the bishop out of the way so White can later move the f-pawn.

2   ...   a7-a6
3   h2-h4

White starts the pawns moving.

3   ...   Kf6-e6

Black is correct to do nothing. He can't accomplish anything by advancing his pawns except to make new targets, so he continues to wait.

4   g2-g4   Ke6-f6
5   Kf2-e3

Now the king starts to advance.

5   ...   e7-e6

No need for this move, which actually makes it easier for White to create a passed pawn. Black could have just played 5 ... Kf6-e6 again.

120

6	g4-g5 check

Pushing the Black king back to his second rank.

6	...	Kf6-e7
7	d4-d5!	

Now White creates a passed pawn.

7	...	e6xd5
8	e4xd5	Bb5-c4
9	Ke3-e4	

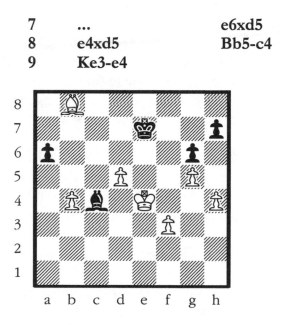

Diagram 71: Black on move

Black now faces a problem. White has a passed pawn on the d-file, and the possibility of creating another passed pawn, eventually playing f4-f5 and using his three versus two majority of pawns on the kingside. Where should Black best place his bishop to meet these threats?

> **PLACING THE DEFENDING BISHOP**
> In bishops of opposite color endgames, the best place
> for the defending bishop is on a diagonal where it can
> thwart two threats at the same time.

In this position, Black needs to get his bishop to the h3-c8 diagonal. Along that diagonal, it stops the passed pawn from crossing the square d7, and also stops White from pushing his f-pawn to f5. If Black can get his bishop to, say, f5, and his king to a square like c6, where it guards d7 and also keeps the White king out of the queenside, Black should be able to draw the game. At the very least, it will be up to White to find a clever winning idea. As the defender in a difficult position, you have to put as many problems as possible in your opponent's way.

	9	...	Bc4-b5

Black heads for the key diagonal via b5 and d7. He could also have moved his bishop to f1 and h3, with the same idea.

	10	Ke4-e5

White needs to operate with multiple threats. From this square, White's king can penetrate to the king-side through the f6 square, or to the queen-side via d6. Black's king on e7 is perfectly situated to keep the White king out (for now).

	10	...	Bb5-d7

So far, Black has all entrance routes covered.

	11	Bb8-d6 check!

White repositions his bishop, driving the Black king off e7. Putting the pawn on this square would be a mistake. Then the squares c6 and e6 would be available for the Black pieces. Don't be in a hurry to push your pawns until you can see the winning idea.

11	...	Ke7-f7

No choice here. If the White king gets into f6 and g7, he will win the Black h-pawn, which should be decisive. With the Black king on f7, however, the White king should be able to enter the Black queen-side via d6.

12	Bd7-c5

A good spot for the bishop, which gets out of the king's way so it can penetrate to d6. It also keeps the Black king off the squares e7 and f8, and effectively penned in the corner.

12	...	Bd7-f5?

The bishop stays on the key diagonal, but this is actually a tactical error. The bishop wants to guard f5 but not actually sit on f5. White's next move shows the problem with this play.

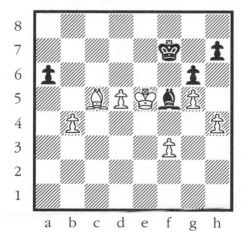

Diagram 72: White on move

123

13   h4-h5!

If Black's bishop were somewhere else on the diagonal, this move wouldn't be possible. Now the g6 pawn has to guard the bishop, so it can't capture. As a result, White gets to capture and create a new weakness on g6. Several moves later in the game, you'll see how important this is.

13   ...   Bf5-d7

The bishop gets off f5, but the damage has been done.

14   h5xg6 check   h7xg6

Now White is one step closer to creating a passed pawn on the kingside. At some future point, the move f4-f5 might break through Black's position.

15   f3-f4

White is planning to move his king over to the queenside to attack Black's pawn on a6, but first he moves his f-pawn into launch position.

15   ...   Bd7-f5

Now there's no harm in locating the bishop on this square.

16   Ke5-d6

The king heads for the weak pawn on a6. In addition, it will support the d-pawn's advance.

16   ...   Kf7-e8

The king prepares to stop the d-pawn.

| 17 | Kd6-c7 | Bf5-e4 |

Forces the pawn forward, so it no longer guards e6 and c6.

| 18 | d5-d6 |

Threatens to queen the pawn, so Black's bishop must retreat to guard d7.

| 18 | ... | Be4-f5 |

Everything under control for now.

| 19 | Kc7-b7 |

Goes after the a-pawn, pulling the bishop off f5.

| 19 | ... | Bf5-d3 |

The only move.

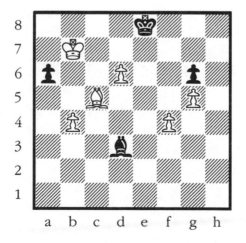

Diagram 73: White on move

Now what? If White's king goes back to c7, the bishop retreats to f5. Black has all danger points covered, but he's stretched his resources to the limit. If White can open another front, Black may collapse. Is there another front to be opened?

20   f4-f5!!

Yes, indeed. This breakthrough moves leaves Black facing some unpleasant choices. If he captures with the pawn, White will have a passed pawn at g6 ready to advance. If he captures with the bishop, White will take the pawn on a6, then win Black's bishop for his advancing b-pawn.

Breakthrough sacrifices like this are a common way of making progress in these apparently blocked endgames. Learn to spot them in advance. And notice that if Black still had a pawn on h7, this idea wouldn't work so well. That's why Black's mistake on move 12 was so important.

20   ...   g6xf5

Black is in big trouble either way; he elects to take with the pawn, getting a passed pawn of his own.

21   Kb7-c7!

White goes back to c7, threatening to push the d-pawn through once more. The Black bishop has to get back to guard d7, but now there's only one way, since Black's f5-pawn now blocks the other diagonal.

21   ...   Bd3-b5

Forced. Now the d-pawn is stopped.

22   g5-g6!

More problems. The new passed pawn lunges for g8.

22   ...   f5-f4

No other plays. If Black tries 22 ... Ke8-f8, White plays 23 d6-d7 discovered check (that bishop on c5!) and then 24 d7-d8 (Q). Meanwhile, the bishop is tied down to d7 and the a-pawn can't move.

23   g6-g7

White will sacrifice the g-pawn to lure the Black king away, exchange his own d-pawn for the Black bishop, then capture the a-pawn and finally queen his last pawn (the b-pawn) for the victory.

23	...	Ke8-f7
24	d6-d7	Bb5xd7
25	Kc7xd7	Kf7xg7
26	Kd7-c6	Kg7-f6
27	Kc6-b6	Kf6-e6
28	Kb6xa6	Ke6-d7

There's no point in pushing the f-pawn since the White bishop securely controls f2.

29	b4-b5	Kd7-c7
30	Ka6-a7	

White controls the queening square, so the b-pawn just marches through.

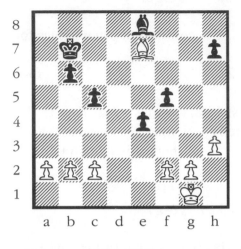

Diagram 74: White on move

In Diagram 74 White is only one pawn ahead, but he has good chances to win. On the queenside, his extra pawn (three pawns against two) will eventually produce a passed pawn. On the kingside, Black's advanced pawns can be attacked by White's king, which might eventually produce another passed pawn. If White can get two widely separated passed pawns, he'll win. As you saw in the last example, the defender can set up a blockade against one pawn, but two separate attacks can overwhelm him. That's what White must try for.

1   Kg1-h2

First, as always, White centralizes his king.

Black intends to bring his king over to the kingside, to oppose White's king. But first he puts his pawns on white squares, so White's bishop can't attack them. Black has calculated that he has time to get to e6 just when he has to.

2   Kh2-g3   Kb7-c8

Now the king heads for e6.

3	Kg3-f4	Kc8-d7

Black gains a move by attacking the loose White bishop.

4	Be7-b4	Kd7-e6

Black's king now guards the weak f-pawn.

In general, a bishop can't guard a mass of pawns against the attack of an opposing king. As the defender in these endings, your king needs to fight off the attack of the enemy king. If White can outmaneuver Black's king, and get his own king to the sector defended by the Black bishop, he'll win. That idea is the basis of his whole plan.

5	Bb4-c3	

The powerful White bishop now keeps the Black king out of e5 and f6.

White now threatens Kf4-g5-h6, attacking the weak h-pawn. Black's king will need to get back to defend that area, so the bishop will have to help defend the f-pawn.

5	...	Be8-d7

When the king moves, the bishop will also guard the f-pawn.

6	g2-g3	

A waiting move. The White pawns on the king-side will eventually have to move to g3 and h4, so that the bishop can't attack them.

129

| 6 | ... | b6-b5 |

Played for a similar reason.

| 7 | Kf4-g5 | Ke6-f7 |
| 8 | h3-h4 | Bd7-c8 |

The bishop keeps guarding the f-pawn.

| 9 | Kg5-h6 | Kf7-g8 |

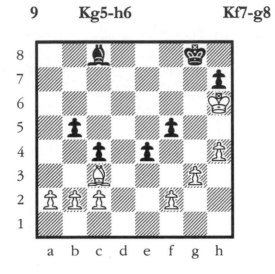

Diagram 75: White on move

The first part of the endgame is over. White has penetrated with his king, driving Black's king out of the center and over to the corner of the board. Now White has to create some threats elsewhere. He'll start by trying to make a passed pawn on the queenside, where he has a majority of pawns.

| 10 | b2-b3 | c4xb3 |

No choice for Black.

130

11	c2xb3

This is the right way for White to recapture. The idea is to eventually get a passed pawn as far away from the kingside as possible. By recapturing this way, White hopes to follow up with a2-a4, getting a passed pawn on the a-file.

If White played instead a2xb3, then he'd later play c2-c4, and after Black recaptured, White would have a passed pawn on the c-file, closer to the center and therefore easier for Black to catch.

Remember that the idea for the winning side in endgames is to create multiple threats as far apart as possible. That puts the maximum strain on the opponent's defenses.

11	...	Bc8-d7

Since White was threatening to create a passed pawn with a2-a4, Black moves to prevent this. Now White will lose a pawn if he plays a2-a4.

Black, on the other hand, is starting to run out of moves. His bishop is tied now to d7, the only square where it both guards the f5-pawn and stops a2-a4. The king is stuck on g8, protecting the h-pawn. None of Black's pawns can move without being captured. If White can figure out a way to apply just a little more pressure, Black's fragile position may collapse.

12	Bc3-e5

Just a waiting move, but a waiting move can be excellent strategy when your opponent has run out of moves. Now what?

12	...	Bd7-e8

Since the f-pawn wasn't attacked yet, Black surrenders his guard on f5. There was no other choice, since he can't afford to give White a passed pawn on the a-file if he can possibly avoid it.

13   Kh6-g5!

White takes advantage of Black's last move. By attacking the f-pawn, White's able to transfer his king from h6 to f6 before Black's king can get to f7 and block.

13   ...   Be8-d7

The only move to both save the f-pawn and keep a2-a4 stopped.

14   Kg5-f6

The White king is now on the loose, headed for e7 and d6 and the queenside.

14   ...   Kg8-f8

The only move to keep the king out.

15   Be5-d6 check!

Chases the king off a key square. If Black plays Kf8-g8, White penetrates the queenside; if Kf8-e8, White comes in on the kingside.

15   ...   Kf8-g8

If White picks off the h-pawn, it's all over quickly as the White h-pawn zips through.

16   Kf6-e7   Bd7-c6

132

Black continues to stop a2-a4.

17   Ke7-e6

With the bishop pushed off the crucial d7 square, White attacks the f-pawn one more time and now Black can't defend it.

17	...	Kg8-g7
18	Ke6xf5	

Black gives up. White's next plan is to get the king over to b4, after which he can play a2-a4 with a passed pawn on the a-file, which will eventually win Black's bishop.

Once the attacker's king can penetrate to the side of the board where the defender's king isn't, the win generally becomes pretty easy.

8

BISHOP AGAINST KNIGHT

So far we've looked at endings where a knight battled against another knight, or a bishop against another bishop. In this chapter we'll see how to play endings where one side's bishop confronts the other side's knight.

FIRST WORD

The knight and the bishop are very different pieces, with different strengths and weaknesses. Here you'll learn how to use them against each other.

STRENGTHS AND WEAKNESSES

The knight and the bishop are very different pieces, with different strengths and weaknesses. In the majority of typical endings, the bishop is a slightly better piece than the knight. But in a significant number of endings, the knight can be better, depending on the pawn structure. Here's a list of the different factors in the endgame that can favor the knight or the bishop.

When you see that an ending is going to involve a knight versus bishop struggle, you have to work to obtain advantages for your side. If you can anticipate the upcoming ending sooner than your opponent, you'll have a big advantage, because you'll be able to steer toward the position you need.

The great masters use this strategy all the time, often simplifying from difficult middle games to simple, and easily won endgames. With a little foresight, you can win this way too!

Now let's look at some endings where knights fight bishops. We'll start with some that favor the knight.

KNIGHTS OR BISHOPS IN THE ENDGAME

- Pawns on both sides of the board: favors the long-range powers of the bishop.
- Pawns all on one side of the board: favors the short-range maneuvering power of the knight.
- The bishop's side has pawns on the same color of the bishop: strongly favors the knight if the pawns are blocked. If not, the bishop will be okay.
- Passed pawns: easily stopped by the bishop from a distance; can be stopped by the knight, but more difficult.
- With a knight, try to eliminate pawns on one side of the board, forcing play into a smaller area where the knight's short range will be an asset rather than a deficit. Try to force your opponent's pawn onto the color squares that his bishop uses. This weakens the bishop and may open avenues of invasion along the squares of opposite color.
- With a bishop, try to keep pawns on both sides of the board with a wide-open, unblocked position. Look to create a passed pawn which will tie down both your opponent's king and knight.

HOW TO WIN WITH THE KNIGHT

In close quarters, the knight can be a formidable opponent, while the bishop's long-range powers are mostly wasted. Take a look at the next position:

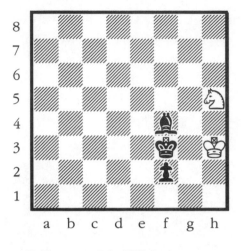

Diagram 76: White on move

White's apparently dead lost in this position. The Black pawn is threatening to queen next turn, the White king can't reach it, and what good is the knight? If White plays Nh5xf4, Black just queens his pawn with a quick mate to follow.

It sounds so hopeless that many players might resign in White's position. But don't! The game can be saved thanks to the short-range power of the knight, and some alertness for possible stalemating opportunities. Watch.

1   Nh5-g3!!

The only move that actually stops the pawn from queening also saves the game. The first point is that if Black plays 1 ... Bf4xg3, White is stalemated. So what can Black do?

1   ...   Bf4-e5

Black tries to gain a little time by shuffling his bishop around. Now White has to be careful. If he plays 2 Kh3-g2, Black wins after 2 ... Be5xg3. So White must play

2	Ng3-f1	Kf3-e2
3	Kh3-g2	Be5-f4

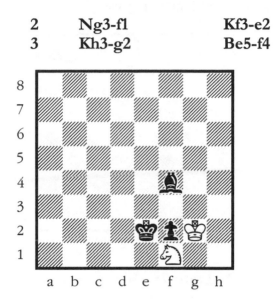

Diagram 77: White on move

Now it looks like White is cooked. If the knight moves, Black will take it off with his bishop, then queen the pawn.

4	Kg2-h1!!

A new position. Now if Black takes the knight with his king, White is again stalemated. How long can this go on?

4	...	Ke2-f3
5	Nf1-g3!	

White is stalemated, no matter which piece takes the knight.

5	...	Bf4-e3
6	Kh1-h2	

Black agrees to a draw, because as long as White's king stays in the corner he can't make progress.

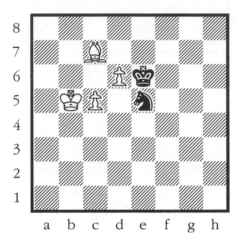

Diagram 78: White on move

White has two extra pawns, connected and passed, and you might think that White wins easily. You'd be wrong! Once again the knight shows its power in close quarters.

1   c5-c6

A good move but actually forced. If White made any other play, Black could reply with 1 ... Ke6-d7 followed by 2 ... Ne5-c6. Black would then draw by leaving his king on d7 and hopping his knight to and from c6 using the squares e5, d4, b8, d8, and b4, as available. White's king and bishop could attack some of these squares but never control all of them.

Blockades like this are the defender's best threat when the bishop lets its pawns get locked on squares of the same color as the bishop. Watch for that!

1   ...   Ke6-d5!

The king launches a counterattack on the pawn on c6, now trapped on a White square. There's no saving that pawn, so White will need to queen his d-pawn.

2	d6-d7	Ne5xc6

Stopping the d-pawn, at least temporarily.

3	Kb5-b6

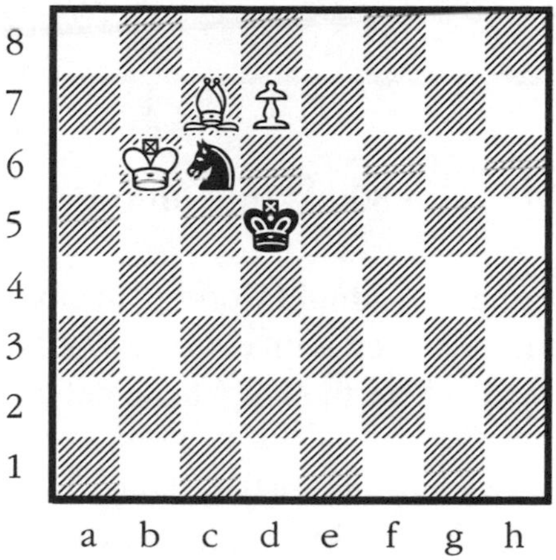

Diagram 79: Black on move

Now what? If Black moves his king, he loses his knight and the game. If he moves his knight, the pawn queens. Black doesn't have any other pieces, so what's he to do? The answer is a shocker...

3	...	Nc6-d8!!
4	Bc7xd8	Kd5-d6

The knight gave itself up to block the pawn for a turn, and now White can't get his king in position fast enough. Next turn Black plays Kd6xd7, with a draw.

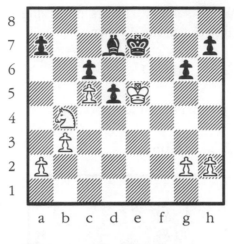

Diagram 80: White on move

In the last two examples, a knight working in close quarters was able to draw against a bishop with extra pawns. Now we'll take a look at an example where the knight can defeat the bishop.

In Diagram 80, there are pawns on both sides of the board, which normally favors the bishop. But Black's pawns in the center are fixed on the same color as the bishop (giving Black what's called a "bad" bishop), and White's pieces have occupied more aggressive squares. Those advantages are enough for the knight to win.

1   Nb4-c2

First job is to put the pieces where they belong, then look for a breakthrough with the pawns. The White king couldn't be better placed; the knight is headed for d4, where he attacks c6 and also gets out of the way for a breakthrough with b4-b5.

1   ...   Bd7-e8

Once the pawns get fixed on the same color squares as the bishop, the bishop is often reduced to complete passivity. Since the king has to stay at e7 to prevent an invasion by the White king, the bishop is stuck guarding the c-pawn.

2	b3-b4

White starts to move the queenside pawns.

2	...	Be8-d7
3	Nc2-d4	

The knight reaches the unassailable square d4. For a knight to show its real power in these endings, it must find a secure square in the center from which it can threaten both wings.

3	...	Bd7-e8
4	a2-a4	

Threatening b4-b5, creating a passed pawn on the c-file.

4	...	a7-a6

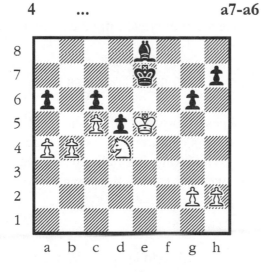

Diagram 81: White on move

5   a4-a5!

A beautiful move, showing a real understanding of the ending. White is ready to play b4-b5 as a sacrifice, opening a line for either his a-pawn or his c-pawn to move forward. To prepare this breakthrough, he first advances his a-pawn as far as possible.

5   ...   Be8-d7

Black's bishop is completely tied to the defense of the c-pawn.

6   b4-b5!

This was the idea behind White's previous move. If Black captures with the a-pawn, White plays 7 a5-a6 Bd7-c8 8 Nd4xc6 check, and Black's pawns will all go. If Black doesn't capture at all, White can just play 7 b5xa6 or b5xc6 (depending on Black's move) with a pretty easy win. Black opts for his best try.

6   ...   c6xb5

This move has the merit of preventing the a-pawn from advancing, at the cost of the d-pawn.

7   Ke5xd5

Black now has a passed b-pawn, but it's no real threat. From d4, the knight can always capture the pawn if it gets as far as b3. Meanwhile, the White king can help push the c-pawn, which will open up an avenue to attack the pawn on a6.

7   ...   Bd7-e8

The bishop has to guard c6 to keep the White king out.

142

8	Nd4-c2

Another repositioning. The knight is headed for b4, where it will do two duties: attacking a6 and c6.

8	...	Be8-d7
9	Nc2-b4	

Now Black's a-pawn can only be defended at the cost of giving up control of c6.

9	...	Bd7-c8
10	Kd5-c6	

The White king immediately marches in. Notice that with all the activity confined to one segment of the board, the bishop's power is wasted while the knight can always maneuver to the optimal attacking squares.

10	...	Ke7-d8

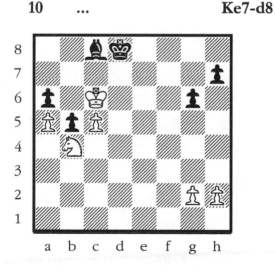

Diagram 82: White on move

11   Kc6-d6!

Excellent technique by White. In the endgames, you sometimes have to count out certain variations and see if they lead directly to a win or a loss. White could have played his king over to b6 and captured the a-pawn, but that variation would actually lose! Here's how play would have gone: 11 Kc6-b6 g6-g5 (or any other waiting move) 12 Nb4xa6 Bc8xa6 13 Kb6xa6 b5-b4! 14 Ka6-b7 b4-b3 15 a5-a6 b3-b2 16 a6-a7 b2-b1(Q) check! Black would get a queen first, and with check. The Black queen would eventually make her way up the board and capture the White pawn on a7, after which Black would win.

Even when an endgame has been going well, as this one has for White, you have to look for traps and tactics. Many a fine game has been spoiled at the very end by carelessness.

What White has actually done is improve the position of his king with the maneuver Kd5-c6-d6. Now he's prepared to advance the c-pawn in perfect safety.

11   ...   Bc8-b7

Holding on to a6.

12	c5-c6	Bb7-c8
13	c6-c7 check	Kd8-e8

With the pawn on the seventh rank, Black is running out of room. Now White heads back, this time to capture the a6-pawn in safety.

14	Kd6-c6	Ke8-f7
15	Kc6-b6	Kf7-e7
16	Nb4xa6	

This capture works now, because White has pushed a pawn up to c7. Now White would queen first, then bring his queen back to capture Black's passed pawn in time. The sequence would be 16 ... Bc8xa6 17 Kb6xa6 b5-b4 18 c7-c8 (Q) b4-b3 19 Qc8-c3 and White captures the b-pawn next turn.

16	...	Ke7-d6
17	Na6-b4	

Black gives up. His own pawn is blockaded again, while he can't stop the combination of White's a-pawn and c-pawn.

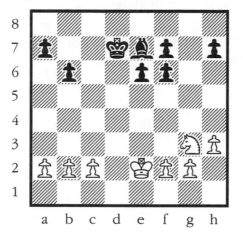

Diagram 83: White on move

Diagram 83 shows a position from a game between Reshevsky and Woliston, played in the U.S. Championship tournament in 1940. Sammy Reshevsky was a leading contender for the World Championship during the 1940s and 1950s, and is considered to be the second strongest American player of all time, behind Bobby Fischer.

Both sides have six pawns, and the position is wide-open, with pawns spread across the whole board. At first glance, this might seem to favor the bishop, especially since, unlike the last game, the pawns are not blockaded or fixed on dark-colored squares.

White, however, has a number of small advantages in Diagram 83. First, he has a majority of pawns on the queenside: three pawns against two. Eventually, this majority will produce a useful passed pawn. Black also has an isolated pawn (on h7) which will prove to be a weakness, and doubled pawns on the f-file. The problem with doubled pawns is that they make Black's majority of four pawns against three on the kingside very difficult to use. Black may never produce a passed pawn, and his pawns can become weak objects of attack.

All in all, White has a clear edge in Diagram 83. Let's see how Reshevsky utilizes it.

1   Ke2-d3

A now-familiar idea: White first centralizes his king and improves the position of his pieces.

1   ...   Kd7-c6

Black follows suit.

2   Ng3-e2

Why not centralize the knight at e4? A good question. It's not enough to put the pieces on squares in the center of the board. You must put the pieces on the *right* squares.

On e4 the knight might look well-placed, but it actually has no scope. The Black bishop on e7 controls all the squares the knight might like to move to. Not only that, but Black would be induced to play f6-f5, an excellent move which not only

146

kicks the knight off its post but also puts Black's pawns on the opposite-colored squares from his bishop, which gives the bishop excellent mobility.

Instead, White heads for the much better central square d4. Once the knight reaches d4, Black can only kick it away at the cost of putting his e-pawn on e5, a dark-colored square where it blocks his own bishop.

	2	...	Be7-c5
	3	f2-f4	

The pawn was attacked so it had to move. White is hoping to play g2-g4 and f4-f5, fixing the kingside pawns on dark squares and restricting Black's bishop.

	3	...	b6-b5?

A bad mistake. Now was the time for Black to fight back with 3 ... f6-f5!, making sure his pawns end up on white squares. After that play, the game would most likely be a draw. Now Black starts to get squeezed.

	4	g2-g4!	

Reshevsky doesn't give his opponent a second chance to correct his mistake. He prevents 4 ... f6-f5, which would now lose a pawn after 5 g4xf5 e6xf5 6 Ne2-g3. Meanwhile, White prepares an eventual f4-f5 of his own. If White's plan works, Black's pawns will get stuck on the dark squares, in the way of his own bishop.

	4	...	a7-a6

Black knows that he needs to keep his pawns on white squares.

5	Kd3-e4

The other advantage of g2-g4 is that, with f6-f5 prevented, White has the powerful center square e4 for his king.

5	...	Bc5-f8

This looks passive, but the bishop has no targets in White's position. It retreats to free the square c5 for Black's king.

6	Ne2-d4 check

Attacks the king and supports the coming thrust with f4-f5.

6	...	Kc6-d6
7	Nd4-b3	

This move is the start of a new maneuver. White wants to exchange Black's pawn on b5, both to get a little closer to having a passed pawn on the queenside, and to open up a little more maneuvering room in the center. He's going to play c2-c4 when appropriate, so first he plays his knight to d2 where it will support the pawn.

7	...	Bf8-e7
8	Nb3-d2	Be7-f8

Black doesn't have anything constructive in mind, so he shuttles his bishop back and forth. These maneuvers look pointless, and many beginners in bad endgame positions are tempted to make weakening pawn moves because they look "aggressive". But that's the wrong approach. Often, the best road to get a draw in an inferior position is to just mark time and see if the stronger side can figure out how to construct a win. Reshevsky, however, shows he's up to the task.

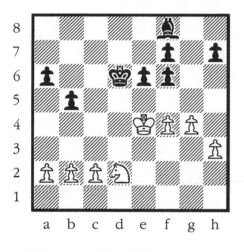

Diagram 84: White on move

9   c2-c4!

Trading off some pawns on the queenside will get White a bit closer to having a passed pawn.

9   ...   Kd6-c5
10   c4xb5   a6xb5

When you're defending, it's a good rule to keep your pawns as far away from the opponent as possible. Black would've done better to play Kc5xb5. Then it would be harder for White to attack the pawn on a6 than it is to get at the pawn on b5.

11   Nd2-b3 check

Having done its job in supporting c2-c4, the knight heads back to its strong position on d4.

In the maneuvering phase of the ending, time is not a key priority. Remember to relocate your pieces to their best positions before launching the critical pawn advances.

11	...	Kc5-d6

Black would like to penetrate the White position, but he can't. Take a look at the next diagram:

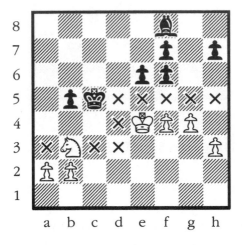

Diagram 85: Black to move out of check

The 'x's show the squares controlled by the White king and the White pawns. Notice that they form an unbroken line extending completely across the board. Even without the help of the White knight, Black can't penetrate White's fortress. Instead of pushing onto c4, where he'd be far away from his own pawns, Black elects to retreat.

12	Nb3-d4

White's ready for the next step: nailing down some kingside weaknesses. Meanwhile, he threatens to pick off the b5-pawn. (If the pawn were still at a6, it would be out of reach.)

12	...	Kd6-c5

Black rushes back to defend.

13   f4-f5!

Now White attacks the pawn on e6, and the Black king can't return to defend because of the weak b5 pawn. Instead, he'll have to push or exchange. Both moves have their problems.

13   ...   e6-e5

Black elects to push. It's a reasonable decision, since after 13 ... e6xf5 14 Nd4xf5, his kingside pawns are all weak and immobile, ideal targets for a nimble little knight. Still, White's happy with the position after e6-e5. After a lot of skillful maneuvering, he's finally fixed the pawns on the color of the Black bishop, which has been his goal all along.

His next job is to start to attack the pawns. This calls for the knight to leave the queenside and head for the kingside.

14   Nd4-f3   h7-h6

Black stops a push with g4-g5, for now.

15   h4-h5

It might seem odd that White is advancing pawns on the side of the board where he has fewer than Black. However, this makes perfect sense here. White is saving his queenside majority for later, when Black's king has had to retreat. If White tried advancing those pawns now, he might get a passed pawn, but Black's long-range bishop would easily stop it, and the pawn could quickly become a liability. Instead, White aims to make progress where Black has less space and more weaknesses.

| 15 | ... | Bf8-e7 |

Still stopping g4-g5.

| 16 | h4-h5! |

This maneuver should now be familiar from the last game. White's going to sacrifice his g-pawn to get a passed pawn that will tie down Black's pieces.

| 16 | ... | Be7-d6 |
| 17 | a2-a3 | |

Before White undertakes decisive action on the kingside, he locks up the queenside, fixing the weak Black pawn on b5. White will return to get that pawn, but not for awhile.

| 17 | ... | Kc5-c4 |

Black tries to invade via c4 and b3. If he tried to prevent the blockade by b5-b4, White would just bypass with 18 a3-a4! getting a passed pawn which would eventually win.

| 18 | Nf3-d2 check! |

White can't permit the Black king to get to b3. Black would then gobble up the queenside pawns and have a winning advantage of his own. In a close endgame, one careless error can easily turn a win into a loss.

| 18 | ... | Kc4-c5 |

The king must retreat.

| 19 | b2-b4 check |

Pushes the king even further back and keeps him locked out of White's side of the board.

After this move, White's two queenside pawns will be fixed on dark squares. That's not a problem, so long as Black's bishop can't penetrate the White position. If the bishop can get in, it could win the pawn on a3, after which White would be in real trouble. Reshevsky has calculated that Black won't have time to move his bishop from d6 to c7 to b6 to d5 to b2, because White's attack on the kingside will come first, and keep the bishop pinned at home. That's true, but he needed to plan out the next few moves carefully.

	19	...	Kc5-c6
	20	Nd2-f3	

The knight did its job keeping the Black king out. Now it's back to the kingside.

	20	...	Bd6-f8

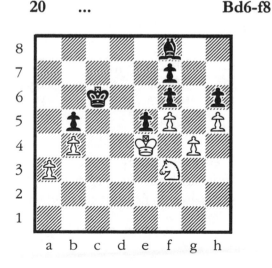

Diagram 86: White on move

153

21   g4-g5!

The breakthrough comes! You should have anticipated this idea after we saw a similar maneuver in the last game. Once again, Black has two ways to capture the pawn, but both come with problems. Taking with 21 ... f6xg5 allows White to snap off the e-pawn and then the f-pawn right away with 22 Nf3xe5 check and 23 Ne5xf7 check. That's clearly not worth considering, so Black will have to take with the h-pawn, but that will give White a passed pawn on the h-file, which will quickly reach h7.

21   ...   h6xg5
22   Nf3-h2

The knight first heads for h4 to back the pawn push to h6.

22   ...   Bf8-g7

To stop the h-pawn, the Black bishop has to get on the diagonal g7-h8. Unfortunately, once it gets there it has no scope for the rest of the game.

23   Nh2-g4   Kc6-d6
24   h5-h6   Bg7-h8
25   h6-h7   Bh8-g7
26   Ng4-h6!

Since the bishop can't move away from h8 without allowing the pawn to queen, this square is open to the knight. Now White threatens to take the pawn on f7, which would win immediately.

26   ...   Kd6-e7

Saving the pawn.

27   Ke4-d5

The Black king has been pulled out of the center, so now White can advance and capture the b-pawn, after which he will push his queenside pawns up the board.

Black gives up. He can't take the knight. If he advances the g-pawn, White takes it with the knight. If he advances the e-pawn, White returns and takes it with his king, then the king goes back to eat the pawn on b5. Black is out of options.

How to Win with the Bishop

We've seen endgames that show the knight to its best advantage; now let's look at some endings that demonstrate the powers of the bishop. As we've said, the bishop is at its best in wide-open positions with pawns on both sides of the board. Our first example shows a routine win for the bishop.

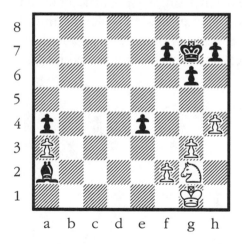

Diagram 87: White on move

Black has four advantages in Diagram 87. He is a pawn ahead; there are pawns on both sides of the board; the position is open, allowing free reign for the bishop; and Black's king will get to a more active position in the center. With careful play, Black can win the game without too much difficulty. He still has to look out for traps, however, because the knight's forking abilities make it a treacherous defensive piece. Let's watch Black's technique.

1   Ng2-e3

As in most endings we've seen, the players start by centralizing their pieces, preparing for operations on both wings. This is a higher priority for the player with the knight, since it takes the knight several moves to get from one side of the board to the other. The bishop can make the journey in one swoop.

1	...	Kg7-f6
2	Kg1-f1	Kf6-e5
3	Kf1-e2	

Black's next decision is simple-should he attack on the queenside or the kingside? The queenside looks inviting, but White has managed to construct a wall there. Take a look at the position if Black plays Ke5-d4 and White replies with Ke2-d2:

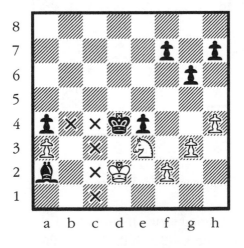

Diagram 88

156

White's king, knight, and a-pawn control all squares marked with an 'x'. As you can see, the squares form a solid wall, keeping out the Black king. To make progress, Black needs to open a second front. That calls for king-side action.

> 3 ... f7-f5!

The right idea. Black plans to create some new, attackable weaknesses on the kingside. Then he'll see how White responds. Notice that all Black's pawns are currently on the same color squares as his bishop. In our last few examples, that's been a big problem for the side with the bishop. What's the difference here?

The answer is that Black's pawns are all still mobile, not fixed in place by White's pawns. As long as the pawns can move, White won't be able to erect a blockade.

> 4 Ne3-c2!

White sets a little trap.

> 4 ... f5-f4!

Black sees the trap and avoids it. If he had tried to invade the queenside with Ke5-d5, White would have played Nc2-b4 check! winning the bishop in the corner.

When you're losing the ending (as White is here) you want to stay alert for traps like this. Once in a while your opponent will walk into them, allowing you to pull out an otherwise lost game.

> 5 g3xf4 check

This creates a weak h-pawn, but if Black captures first, he will create a passed e-pawn which will be strong.

157

| 5 | ... | Ke5xf4 |

Now Black threatens to pick off the h-pawn with Kf4-g4.

| 6 | Nc2-e3 |

White guards g4 with his knight and saves the pawn for now.

| 6 | ... | Ba2-b3 |

A waiting move. White has few moves at his disposal, and will have to lose ground wherever he goes.

| 7 | Ke2-d2 |

The king was the only piece that could move without immediately losing material. But now the Black king reaches f3.

| 7 | ... | Kf4-f3 |
| 8 | Kd2-e1 | |

White's cramped, but he can still keep the Black king out as long as he can shuttle between e1 and f1. Black's next job is to get his bishop to d3.

8	...	Bb3-e6
9	Ke1-f1	h7-h5
10	Kf1-e1	

Any move of the knight lets Black's king get to g4.

10	...	Be3-a2
11	Ke1-f1	Ba2-b1
12	Kf1-e1	Bb1-d3

Mission accomplished. White now has to move, losing either the f-pawn or the h-pawn.

| 13 | Ne3-d5 | Kf3-g4 |
| 14 | Nd5-e7 | Kg4xh4 |

Black doesn't need to worry about the g-pawn. White won't be able to stop the h-pawn without giving up something.

| 15 | Ne7xg6 check | Kh4-g5 |
| 16 | Ng6-e5 | Kg5-f5 |

Chases the knight even farther from the h-file.

| 17 | Ne5-f7 | h5-h4 |

The pawn starts his winning advance and the knight can't get back in time to stop it. If White tries 18 Nf7-h6 check, Black plays 18 ... Kf5-f4! and the knight can't approach the pawn. White will have to pitch his e-pawn to let his king get over.

18	f2-f3	e4xf3
19	Ke1-f2	Kf5-f4
20	Nf7-d6	h4-h3

It's hopeless now, so White gives up.

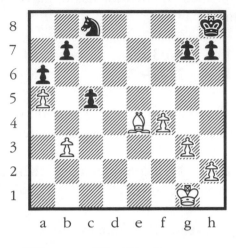

Diagram 89: Black on move

Pawns are even in Diagram 89, but White's doing quite well anyway. His has a potentially active majority of three against two on the kingside, which are mobile and ready to advance. Black has three against two on the queenside, but the b-pawn can't move easily; that's a liability. White's bishop is active, with a center posting and beautiful open lines. Black's knight is off to the side. Both kings are on the first rank, but White has an easier road to the center. All in all, a very solid edge for White with good winning chances.

1 ... Nc8-d6

Black's first move is forced. His b-pawn was attacked by the bishop, and if he tries to save it by 1 ... b7-b5, White has 2 Be4-b7! forking the knight and the a-pawn. On d6, though, the knight has problems. The b-pawn can't move without being lost, so the knight is tied down to protecting it.

> **WATCH OUT FOR IMMOBILE PIECES**
> In the endgame, immobile pieces are a sign of
> impending defeat.

2	Be4-d5

A great spot for the bishop. It keeps the pressure on b7, while preventing the Black king from reaching the center via g8.

2	...	h7-h5

Black tries to get the king into play via h7 and g6. He's hoping to exchange some kingside pawns, to enhance his drawing chances.

3	Kg1-f2

Time to centralize the kings, then search for possibilities.

3	...	Kh8-h7
4	Kf2-e3	Kh7-g6

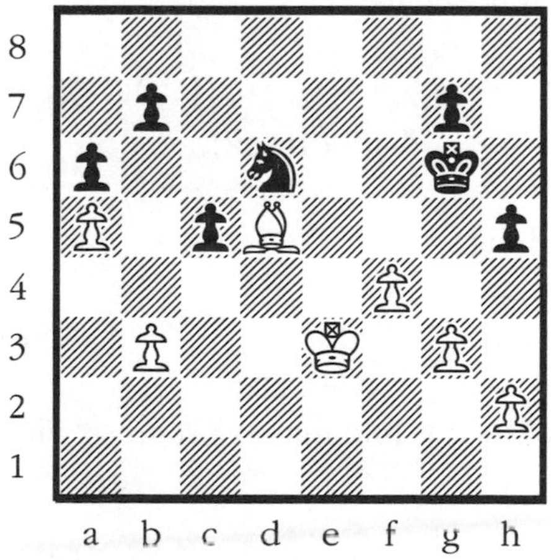

Diagram 90: White on move

White's run into a temporary stall. The Black knight and pawn guard the squares from b4 to e4, so White's king can't make any more forward progress. When the way seems blocked in an endgame, ask yourself if letting your opponent move instead is a good idea. If the defender is running out of moves himself, making him lead may be a way to break through.

5	Bd5-f3!	

Fine play. White attacks the h-pawn, tying down the Black king. Black is now reduced to just two moves: retreating with the king (5 ... Kg6-h6) or advancing the h-pawn. Since retreating doesn't look good, Black chooses to advance.

5	...	h5-h4
6	g3-g4!	

Another good move, which White had foreseen last turn. Taking the pawn (6 g3xh4) is a waste of time, leaving White a pawn ahead, but with weak, doubled pawns that Black could attack. Instead White creates a couple of mobile pawns which will push Black right out of the center.

6	...	Kg6-f6
7	g4-g5 check!	

White keeps pushing.

7	...	Kf6-e6

If Black plays Kf6-f5, White makes progress with 8 h2-h3 and 9 Bf3-g4 check.

8	Bf3-g4 check	Ke6-e7

If Black plays 8 ... Nd6-f5 check, he walks into a pin and loses the knight after White plays 9 Ke3-e4!

9   f4-f5

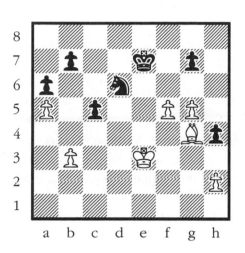

Diagram 91: Black on move

Take a look. White's pawns have rolled forward, grabbing a huge chunk of the center and opening an avenue for White's king to penetrate (e3-f4-e5). Black has to close this avenue, or from e5 and d5 the White king will dominate the board, eventually winning the Black c-pawn.

9   ...   Nd6-f7

Part of a repositioning maneuver. The knight takes over control of e5, while the king will move to d6 to guard d5. Meanwhile, Black attacks the g-pawn.

10   Ke3-f4

Protects the g-pawn.

| 10 | ... | Ke7-d6 |

Guards e5 and d5.

| 11 | Bg4-f3! |

With the knight gone from d6, White goes back to an attack on the weak b-pawn.

| 11 | ... | Nf7-e5 |

Black can't hold everything, so he elects to let the queenside pawns go, in the hope that he can eliminate all the pawns on that side, and draw if the only remaining pawns are on the kingside.

Black didn't play 11 ... Kd6-c7, guarding the b-pawn, probably because he saw the following variation: 12 f5-f6! g7xf6 13 g5-g6! Nf7-h6 (guarding g8) 14 Bf3-d5 followed by g6-g7 and g7-g8, winning the Black knight for the White pawn.

| 12 | Bf3xb7 | c5-c4! |

Trading some pawns.

| 13 | b3xc4 | Ne5xc4 |

Black is hoping White will play 14 Bb7xa6 Nc4xa5, where Black is doing well because all the pawns are on one side of the board, favoring the knight. But White has other ideas.

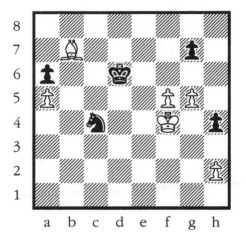

Diagram 92: White on move

14   f5-f6!

A key move. White aims to create a passed pawn quickly.

14   ...   g7-g6

Black sees that White has a clever forced win if he takes the pawn: 14 ... g7xf6; 15 g5-g6 Kd6-e7; 16 g6-g7 Ke7-f7; 17 Bb7-d5 check!, a bishop fork winning the loose knight.

15   Bb7-d5!!

A brilliant piece of tactics which nails down the win.

If Black plays 15 ... Kd6xd5, White just queens his f-pawn. If Black doesn't capture, his pieces will be hopelessly tied down and White will win the a-pawn for free.

Being able to see these little tactical shots a move or two in advance makes winning tough endgame a whole lot easier.

| 15 | ... | Nc4-e5 |

The knight head for d7 to guard f8.

| 16 | f6-f7 | Ne5-d7 |
| 17 | Bd5-c4! | |

The a-pawn falls.

17	...	Kd6-e7
18	Bc4xa6	Ke7xf7
19	Ba6-b7	

Black gives up. He'll have to lose his knight to stop the a-pawn, after which White will win Black's pawns on the kingside.

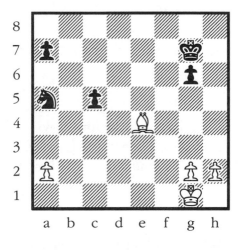

Diagram 93: White on move

This ending is from a game between Boris Spassky and Bobby Fischer, from a tournament in Los Angeles in 1966, six years before their famous match for the World Championship. The pawns are equal, but the position favors the bishop: wide-open lines and pawns on both sides of the board.

Let's see how Spassky takes advantage of his opportunities.

1	h2-h4!

This is a key move in the ending, and shows the need for original thinking, of which Spassky was eminently capable. Usually the first goal in an ending is to centralize the king. Here White sees that he has another positional goal which is more important.

White wants to *fix* the Black pawn at g6 on its current square, so that he can continue to attack it with his bishop. That, in turn, ties down Black's king to defending the pawn. That's good for White.

If White played instead 1 Kg1-f2, Black wouldn't move his king just yet; instead he would play 1 ... g6-g5!, putting the pawn on a Black square and freeing his own king.

White now has a target to attack for the next several moves.

1	...	Na5-c4

Black's knight must get off the edge and into the game.

2	Kg1-f2

With the critical h4 move already played, now it's back to basics: centralize the king.

2	...	Nc4-e5

The knight is now on a strong central square, where it protects the Black pawn (b4, c4, and d4 are all under Black's control) and stops g2-g4 for White.

3	Kf2-e3	Kg7-f6

167

Both sides centralize.

4	Ke3-f4	Ne5-f7

Black is going to try to play g6-g5 check, exchanging off a pair of pawns. The fewer pawns on the board, the easier it will be to draw.

5	Kf4-e3

This looks inconsistent, and it is. Spassky himself said after the game that the right idea was to continue with 5 Be4-d5 g6-g5 check 6 h4xg5 Nf7xg5 7 Bd5-c4, followed by moving his king to the queenside. Even with this slip, White has things under control.

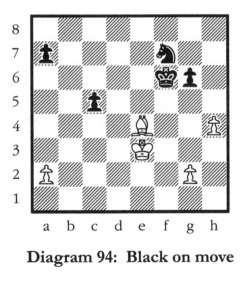

Diagram 94: Black on move

5	...	g6-g5?

Possibly the losing move. Now White gets a strong h-pawn which ties down the Black knight. The quiet move 5 ... Nc7-d6 sets up a defensive structure that was hard to crack.

6	h4-h5!

As we've seen before, the passed pawn can be very strong.

6	...	Nf7-h6

Black can stop the pawn, but his knight is out of play.

7	Ke3-d3

The king goes after the undefended queenside pawns.

7	...	Kf6-e5
8	Be4-a8	

The bishop gets far away from the harassing Black king.

8	...	Ke5-d6

Guards the pawn on c5.

9	Kd3-c4

Now the Black king can't move without losing the pawn.

9	...	g5-g4
10	a2-a4	

This pawn heads for a5.

10	...	Nh6-g8
11	a4-a5	Ng8-h6
12	Ba8-e4	

Next job: get the king to a6 to win the a-pawn or the c-pawn.

12	...	g4-g3
13	Kc4-b5	

Black now has a choice of which pawn to lose.

13	...	Nh6-g8
14	Be4-b1	

So the bishop can't be attacked by the knight.

15	...	Ng8-h6
16	Kb5-a6	Kd6-c6
17	Bb1-a2!	

This is even better than taking the pawn immediately, since now Black doesn't get to advance his c-pawn.

Fischer gave up, since he couldn't prevent White from capturing his a-pawn, then pushing his own.

ROOK AGAINST PAWNS

Suppose you're winning an ending where you have a rook and a single pawn (and a king of course) and your opponent has the same material. Your pawn is farther advanced, so you push it up the board and make a queen. Your opponent naturally gives up his rook

FIRST WORD

When your opponent has just pawns left and you have a rook, you can usually win in the end. Read on to learn how.

for your queen, and you recapture. Now you have a rook left, and he has a pawn.

Can you win this ending? Will your rook and king be able to cooperate, stop his pawn, and finally capture it, or will your opponent be able to draw the game?

Mostly, you should be able to win this endgame, but your rook and king will have to work together efficiently. Let's see how it's done.

Rook Against One Pawn

The battle of a rook against a single pawn can be a close affair. Suppose that White has the rook and Black has just a single pawn. In order to win the game, White's king and rook will have to cooperate. If the White king is close enough so that the king and rook can both control some square that the pawn has to cross, then White can eventually capture the pawn and checkmate with the rook. If White's king is too far away, or if the Black king can somehow fend off the White king, Black can draw the game by queening his pawn and forcing White to exchange his rook for the new queen.

Take a look at Position 95.

Diagram 95: Black on move

The White king and the Black pawn are both racing for the queening square, b1. Can White make it in time? Just barely, but he has to know a couple of tactical tricks to win the game. Let's watch how White handles matters.

1 ...   b5-b4

There's no subtlety in Black's play. He just pushes the pawn as fast as he can.

2 Kg4-f3

172

White heads for b1 by the most direct route.

| 2 | ... | b4-b3 |

Will Black get there first?

| 3 | Kf3-e2 |

If Black now plays 3 ... b3-b2, White moves 4 Ke2-d1, and Black's king has to leave the protection of the pawn. So Black needs to keep the White king at a distance.

| 3 | ... | Kc3-c2! |

Keeps out the White king and threatens to queen the pawn.

| 4 | Rb8-c8 check! |

This is the key maneuver in this ending. White makes progress by checking with his rook, forcing the Black king to give ground.

| 4 | ... | Kc2-b2 |
| 5 | Ke2-d2 | |

Getting closer.

| 5 | ... | Kb2-a2 |

Now the pawn is free to advance again.

| 6 | Kd2-c3 |

Once the White king gets next to the pawn, White's almost home.

| 6 | ... | b3-b2 |
| 7 | Rc8-a8 check | Ka2-b1 |

Black is forced to block his pawn, but he has one last trap.

| 8 | Ra8-b8 |

This ensures the capture of the pawn.

| 8 | ... | Kb1-a1! |

Diagram 96: White on move

Do you see the trap? If White blindly plays 9 Rb8xb2??, Black is stalemated in the corner!

Can White still win? Yes, but he needs one last finesse.

| 9 | Kc3-c2! |

White captures the pawn with check, avoiding stalemate.

| 9 | ... | b2-b1 (Q) check |

174

10	Rb8xb1 check

And White will force checkmate in a few moves.

The win isn't always that tricky. Sometimes White can use his rook to prevent the Black king from helping his pawn. When that happens, the pawn can get in trouble on its own. Take a look at the next position:

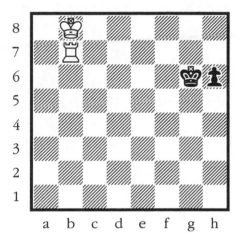

Diagram 97: White on move

White's king is far away, which is a problem for him. But Black's king and pawn are far away from the queening square, which is a really big problem for him. In fact, it allows White to win the game quite easily, if he sees the right idea.

1	Rb7-b5!

Here it is. White controls the entire fifth rank with his rook, so the Black king can't make any progress towards the queening square. That means the pawn will have to make its way on its own, a tough task for a pawn matched up against a powerful rook.

175

1	...	h6-h5

There's no way Black can improve the position of his king, so there's nothing to do but let the pawn march.

2	Kb8-c7	h5-h4
3	Kc7-c6	h4-h3

Once the pawn gets too far from the king, the rook steps in for the kill.

4	Rb5-b3!

Attacking the pawn, which can't be defended.

4	...	h3-h2

Almost!

5	Rb3-h3

That's it. The rook captures the pawn next turn.

Rook Against Two Pawns

When one side has two pawns against a rook, the game becomes considerably more interesting. If the pawns are far enough advanced, they may even defeat a rook!
Take a look at the next position:

Diagram 98: Black on move

Black's king is far away from the action, while the pawns are fairly far advanced. The rook can put up a fight, but eventually the pawns will triumph.

1	...	Ra1-f1

The right idea for Black is to attack the leading pawn. This freezes both pawns in their tracks. If either one moves, Black captures the f-pawn first, then picks up the g-pawn later.

2	Ke3-d4!	

With the pawns immobilized, White brings up the king to assist. By moving to d4, rather than e4, he keeps the Black king blocked out of c3.

2	...	Kb2-b3

Black tries to get the king closer.

Black has another idea which almost works. He could have played 2 ... Rf1-f5, attacking the g-pawn. If the g-pawn advances, Black could take the f-pawn. But White could still win by playing 3 Kd4-e4! Rf5xg5 4 f6-f7, and Black can't reach the queening square.

3	Kd4-e5

Once the White king can support the two pawns, Black is in trouble.

3	...	Kb3-c4
4	g5-g6	

As a rule, if White can get both his pawns to the sixth rank, he can win. That's the case here.

4	...	Rf1-e1 check
5	Ke5-d6	Re1-g1
6	g6-g7	

The pawns advance steadily.

6	...	Kc4-d4

Black is trying to get to the queening squares, but the White king blocks the most direct route.

Diagram 99: White to move

7   Kd6-c6!!

This apparently nonsensical move is actually the only way to win. What's wrong with the obvious 7 Kd6-e6? Black would reply 7 ... Kd4-e4, and then White has a couple of choices:

One idea would be to escort the pawns in with the king, by playing 8 Ke6-f7. But Black would play 8 ... Ke4-e5, attacking the rear pawn with his king, and after 9 g7-g8 (Q) Rg1xg8 10 Kf7xg8 Ke5xf6, Black has managed to exchange off all the pawns and get a draw.

The other idea would be 8 f6-f7, hoping that Black would capture, 8 ... Rg1xg7, after which White queens on f8 with an easy win. But Black wouldn't capture on g7! Instead, he would play 8 ... Rg1-g6 check! White would have to move forward, 9 Ke6-e7, and Black would play 9 ... Rg6xg7, capturing one pawn while pinning another. Next turn he'd capture on f7, again with a draw.

This last variation shows the key to the winning idea, however. White doesn't need his king in the immediate vicinity of the pawns to force a queen – the pawns can do that all by themselves. White has to make sure that when Black checks on g6, White doesn't have to play his king up to the seventh rank. He needs to be able to play back to the fifth rank, so that his pawn on f7 can't get pinned. That means he has to get his king away from Black's king. Hence, the weird-looking move 7 Kd6-c6, aiming to get the king over to b5.

7	...	Kd4-c4!

If White wants to get out to b5, Black has to stop him. The Black king can't help stop the pawns anyway.

8	Kc6-d7!

A new idea — the king heads directly for the square e8, where it can force through the f-pawn. Black is one move too late to stop this plan.

8	...	Kc4-d5
9	Kd7-e8	Kd5-e6
10	f6-f7	

One White pawn will queen, but Black still has a resource.

10	...	Rg1-a1

Diagram 100: White on move

Oops. Has White checkmated himself? If either pawn queens, Black plays Ra1-a8 checkmate. If White tries Ke8-d8, Black plays Ke6xf7 and gobbles up the other pawn with an easy win. What can White do?

11   f7-f8 (N) check!!

This is White's trick. By underpromoting the f-pawn to a knight, he chases the Black king from e6 with a check.

11	...	Ke6-f6
12	g7-g8 (Q)	Ra1-a8 check
13	Ke8-d7	

And White will win.

ROOK & PAWN AGAINST ROOK

These are tricky endgames, but when you learn the examples in this chapter, you'll handle them better than almost anyone you play against, and you'll find yourself turning draws into wins and losses into draws.

FIRST WORD

In this chapter, we'll look at endings where one side has a rook and a lone pawn, while the other side is defending with just a rook.

The basic idea is this: the defender wants to get his king in front of the advancing pawn. If he can do that, he'll mostly get his draw. The winning side tries to use his rook to keep the defender's king cut off from the pawn, either along a file or a rank. If the defender's king can't get to the pawn, he'll mostly lose.

These endings require a surgeon's touch, so study these examples closely.

Defender's King in Front of the Pawn

If you can get your king in front of the enemy pawn, you should be able to draw the game by playing alertly. Let's see just how it's done.

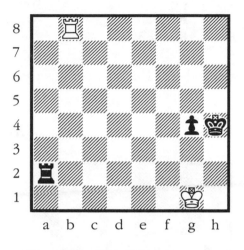

Diagram 101: White on move

Black's pawn is marching down the g-file, but White's king has managed to reach the queening square, g1. Can Black force the pawn through? Not if White knows what he's doing. Here's how White should play to secure the draw:

> **1   Rb8-b3!**

This is the critical idea. White's rook guards the third rank, making it impossible for Black to move his king there. If Black does nothing, White just shuffles his rook along the third rank, holding his position.

What can Black do? He could try checking:

> | 1 | ... | Ra2-a1 check |
> |---|-----|--------------|
> | 2 | Kg1-g2 | Ra1-a2 check |
> | 3 | Kg2-g1 | |

Well, that didn't accomplish much. If he moves his rook along the second rank, White just moves his rook along the third:

3	...	Ra2-c2
4	Rb3-a3	Rc2-b2
5	Ra3-c3	

This isn't going anywhere. The only serious try is to push the pawn.

| 5 | ... | g4-g3 |

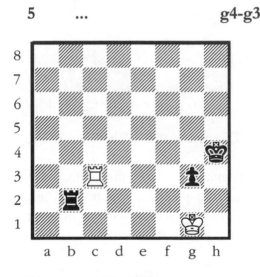

Diagram 102: White on move

Now Black has a real threat. He plans to play Kh4-h3 and Rb2-b1 checkmate. Can you see how to stop this plan?

| 6 | Rc3-c8! | |

This is the other half of White's idea. When Black advances his pawn to the third rank, White moves his rook back to the eighth, and starts giving checks. Because Black's pawn is occupying a key square on the third rank, he won't have anyplace to hide from the checks.

| 6 | ... | Kh4-h3 |

7	Rc8-h8 check!	Kh3-g4
8	Rh8-g8 check	Kg4-f3
9	Rg8-f8 check	Kf3-e4
10	Rf8-e8 check	

Where can Black's king go? There's no hiding spot from the checks. If the king goes back toward the pawn, White just keeps checking. If he tries to run back toward the rook...

10	...	Ke4-d5
11	Re8-g8!	

White just stops the checks and goes back to capture the unde-fended pawn.

11	...	Rb2-b3
12	Kg1-g2!	

Next turn White captures the pawn with his rook and the game is a draw.

White started out controlling the third rank with his rook to prevent Black from moving his king there, creating checkmating threats. Once Black was forced to put his pawn on the third rank, he had no hiding places from the checks.

Defender's King is Cut Off

If you're the player with the extra pawn, and you can stop your opponent's king from getting in front of your pawn, you'll probably be able to win.

Take a look at the next position, and I'll show you the right way to play:

Diagram 103: Black on move

White's got an extra pawn in Diagram 103. Black's going to try and block the pawn with his king.

> 1 ... Kd7-e7

The king heads for f7 and g7, blocking the pawn. What should White do? There's only one good move.

> 2 Ra2-f2!

This is it! The rook takes up position on the f-file, cutting off the Black king. Now the Black king can never reach g8, so Black will have to stop the pawn with his rook. That's much more difficult.

> 2 ... Rg8-h8 check

White was threatening to play Kh5-h6 and g5-g6. Black tries to keep White from moving his pawn by checking the king.

> 3 Kh5-g6!

The White king blocks the pawn, but this is just temporary. White has a two-stage plan to win:

First, use the king to push the Black rook out of the way. This will allow White to get his king to g8 and his pawn to g7.

Second, use his rook to help extricate the king from in front of the pawn, allowing the pawn to push through to queen.

Black can't stop this plan, although he can make things difficult for White. Let's see how play would proceed.

> 3   ...   Rh8-g8 check

Black keeps checking.

> 4   Kg6-h6

White can't play Kg6-h7, because Black would then take White's pawn. The king and pawn have to work together.

> 4   ...   Rg8-h8 check
> 5   Kh6-g7!

The decisive move for this part of the plan. The king grabs control of the squares in front of the pawn, forcing the Black rook to run away.

187

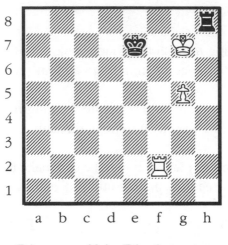

Diagram 104: Black on move

5	...	Rh8-h1

The rook can't stay in front of the pawn any longer. Instead he moves behind the pawn, and tries to annoy White by checking from the rear.

It's now easy for White to get his pawn to the seventh rank with his king in front of it. The next few moves go like this:

6	g5-g6	Rh1-h3

There's no point in moving the Black king. Actually it's doing a good job where it is, guarding the squares f6, f7, and f8, and preventing the White king from moving in that direction.

7	Kg7-g8	Rh3-h1
8	g6-g7	Rh1-h3

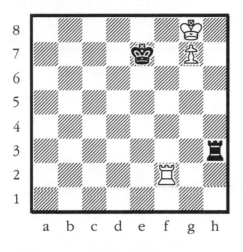

Diagram 105: White on move

Now what? White's king is blocked from moving by the Black rook and the Black king, and White's pawn can't advance until the king can extricate itself somehow. The next part of the plan is up to the rook.

> **9   Rf2-f4!**

This is the key move for White. What he's doing is called "building a bridge". By putting the rook on the fourth rank, he'll be able to use it to block a check in a few moves.

> **9   ...   Rh3-h1**

Black can only await developments.

> **10   Rf4-e4 check!**

This is the other key move. Up to now the rook has held its position on the f-file to keep the Black king cut off from the pawn.

With the pawn on the seventh rank, however, White can actually let the king approach if he wishes.

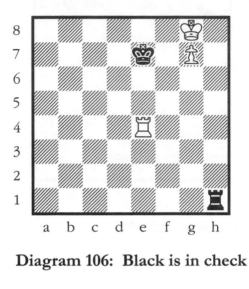

Diagram 106: Black is in check

10	...	Ke7-d7

Black would like to move over and attack the pawn, but that gives White a very easy win since the Black king himself blocks the f-file. After 10 ... Ke7-f6, White just plays 11 Kg8-f8! and his pawn queens next turn. Instead, Black has to move one more file away from the pawn. Now the king doesn't control f7 any longer, so the White king can emerge from his grotto.

11	Kg8-f7!

Now White threatens to queen the pawn, so Black needs to start checking.

11	...	Rh1-f1 check
12	Kf7-g6	Rf1-g1 check
13	Kg6-f6	Rg1-f1 check
14	Kf6-g5	

190

Can White ever get away from these checks?

14	...	Rf1-g1 check

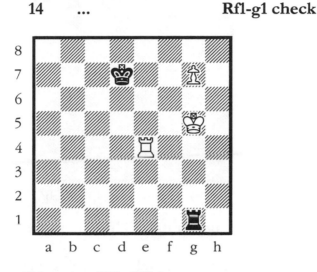

Diagram 107: White on move

15	Re4-g4!

Yes, indeed! Now we can see why White put the rook on the fourth rank back on his ninth move. He's able to use it as a blocker to stop the checks. Since Black can't prevent White from queening his pawn next turn, he gives up.

This is a key endgame, so play through it a few times and make sure you understand White's entire maneuver. White can run into some problems if his pawn is very far back. Take a look at the next position:

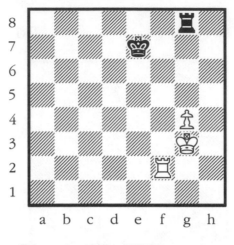

Diagram 108: White on move

This looks like the previous problem. Black's king is cut off from the pawn by the White rook at f2. Black's rook stops the White pawn now, but the White king is ready to assist it.

However, it's crucially different in one respect: the White pawn is only on the fourth rank, not the fifth as before. And just that small difference allows Black to draw the game. Watch what happens when White tries to advance his pawn.

1	Kg3-h4	Rg8-h8 check
2	Kh4-g5	

As before, the White king moves in front of its pawn to try and clear the way.

2	...	Rh8-g8 check
3	Kg5-h5	Rg8-h8 check
4	Kh5-g6	Rh8-g8 check

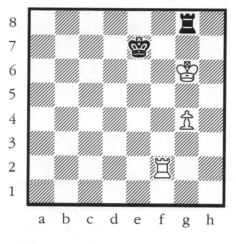

Diagram 109: White on move

Notice the problem. If White continues to push his king forward, he loses the pawn behind it. The only way White can keep his pawn is to retreat by Kg6-h5, but then Black just keeps checking forever. That extra rank between the White pawn and the Black rook gave Black just enough space to let him keep checking at a safe distance.

Defender's King Cut Off by Three Files

White can win some positions with a pawn on the fourth rank, but in order to do so, the Black king has to be cut off by at least three files. The reason is that White will need to use his rook to help advance the pawn (the last example showed why the king can't do this alone) and while the rook is helping, the Black king will creep closer. The White rook has to help the pawn but still have time to keep the Black king at least one file away at the end.

The next position shows the idea:

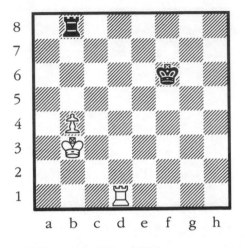

Diagram 110: White on move

Knowing he has to buy himself some time later on, White starts by keeping the enemy king as far away as possible.

1   Rd1-e1!

Now the Black king is three files away from the White pawn.

1   ...   Kf6-f5

Black's rook is currently on the best possible square, where it stops the pawn from as great a distance as possible. A move like 1 ... Rb8-b7?, which shortens the distance between the White pawn and the Black rook, just makes White's job easier.

2   Kb3-c4

With the enemy king cut off, the White king makes its move up the board.

2   ...   Rb8-c8 check

Black starts his delaying checks.

| 3 | Kc4-d5! |

White steps to the center, away from his own pawn. In the previous position, White didn't have this option because the Black king was too close.

| 3 | ... | Rc8-b8 |

There's no point in further checks, because the White king will just continue to advance. (There's no pawn behind the king for White to be concerned about.) Instead, Black just returns to attacking the pawn. If White retreats with 4 Kd5-c5, Black can start checking again.

| 4 | Re1-b1! |

Not this time! The rook lifts its blockade of the Black king to help push the pawn forward.

| 4 | ... | Kf5-f6 |

The rook can't stop the pawn alone. If Black plays 4 ... Rb8-b5 check, White has 5 Kd5-c6, and the pawn moves next turn.

| 5 | b4-b5 | Kf6-e7 |
| 6 | Kd5-c6! | |

White's careful not to get outflanked. If he blindly played 6 b5-b6, Black would move 6 ... Ke7-d7, and his king would get in front of the pawn.

| 6 | ... | Ke7-d8 |
| 7 | b5-b6 | Kd8-c8 |

195

Diagram 111: White on move

The king got in front of the pawn, but the cost was too high: Black's rook is immobilized.

8   Rb1-h1!

The threat is 9 Rh1-h8 checkmate, and Black can't do much about it.

Cutting Off the Defender on the Rank

There's another way for White to win these endings besides keeping the Black king cut off on one side of the board. It's also possible to isolate Black's king on a rank, so that the problem of guarding the queening square falls entirely on the Black rook. This method can only be tried if the Black king has penetrated deeply into White's half of the board which makes it less common than the approach we've seen so far. Take a look at Position 112 on the next page.

Diagram 112: White on move

White's pawn is on the second rank; that's not good for his winning chances. If he tries to cut the king off with 1 Rh7-d7, Black's king will still be close enough to secure an eventual draw.

But White has another plan of attack. Black's king has wandered far into enemy territory. Watch White take advantage.

> **1   Rh7-h4!**

White moves the rook back and seizes control of the fourth rank. Now the Black king is confined to the box of squares from d3 to h1. Once White gets his pawn marching, the king won't be able to get anywhere close to the b8 square.

> **1   ...   Ke3-d3**

The king tries to be as close to the White pawn as possible.

> **2   Rh4-a4!**

This is the second part of White's maneuver. By moving to a4, the rook creates a little pocket of safety for the king to move off the first rank. If White didn't make this play, the Black rook would keep checking the king when it emerged from b1.

2	...	Rb8-h8

Black can't stop the escaping king; he'll try to pin the b2 pawn.

3	Kb1-a2	Rh8-h2

Pins the pawn and prevents it from advancing.

4	Ra4-g4	

White keeps the rook on the fourth rank, but moves it away from a4 so the king can advance along with the pawn.

4	...	Rh2-f2
5	Ka2-a3	

This step unpins the pawn on b2; it's now free to move to b8.

5	...	Rf2-f1
6	b2-b4	Kd3-c3

The Black king gets closer, but it's still cut off by the White rook. Now, however, Black has a threat: • Rf1-a1 checkmate!

7	Ka3-a4	

White avoids the threat and keeps the king and pawn moving forward.

7	...	Rf1-a1 check

8	Ka4-b5	Ra1-a8

The rook is useless behind the pawn; it moves back in front. But without the help of the Black king, it can't do much.

9	Rg4-g3 check

This chases the Black king away from attacking the pawn.

9	...	Kc3-d4
10	Kb5-c6!	

White reaches a key square, where he both blocks out the Black king, assists his pawn, and chases away the Black rook.

10	...	Ra8-c8 check
11	Kc6-b7	Rc8-c1
12	b4-b5	Kd4-c5
13	b5-b6	Rc1-b1
14	Rg3-g6!	

Diagram 113: Black on move

The rook move is the final stroke. The pawn is now protected, and the Black king is still cut off, this time on the sixth rank. The pawn will march on to b8 and the rook won't be able to stop it.

ROOK & PAWNS AGAINST ROOK & PAWNS

If your rook is active (attacking enemy pawns, pushing your passed pawns up the board, and restricting the enemy king) you'll have real chances to win, even if you don't have any extra pawns.

FIRST WORD

When rook and pawns battle against rook and pawns, one feature dominates the game – an active rook.

If your rook is passively defending, you're in real trouble. It's going to be hard to win, even if you are a pawn ahead, and you may even lose.

Your top priority in these endings is simple: activate your rook, and keep your opponent on the defensive!

The Power of an Outside Pawn

When there are pawns on both sides of the board and you have an extra pawn, in most cases, you'll be able to win the game if you play well.

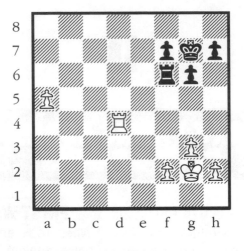

Diagram 114: Black on move

Position 114 is taken from the 34th match game between Alexander Alekhine and Jose Capablanca in 1927. Capablanca had been World Champion in 1927. In this dramatic game, he lost the title to Alekhine, who went on to hold the title (with one brief interruption) until his death in 1946.

In the position, Alekhine has an extra passed pawn on the a-file. In addition, his rook is very well placed, able to get to a4 behind his pawn and push it up the board. In an ending like this, you're a lot better off if you can guard your pawn from the rear (squares like a4, a3, a2, or a1) than from the side (d5) or the front (a8 or a7).

Once your rook is behind the pawn, your opponent has to physically block the pawn by putting one of his pieces (probably the rook) in front of it. As your pawn goes farther up the board, the scope of your rook increases and the scope of your opponent's rook decreases. That's good for you.

What is Alekhine's winning plan? Basically, it consists of six steps:

> **(1)** Put his rook behind his pawn — very important. Black will then have to block the a-pawn with his rook.
>
> **(2)** Move his king to the center of the board.
>
> **(3)** If Black leaves his king on the king's side of the board, attack the Black rook which will be stopping the a-pawn.
>
> **(4)** If Black moves the king to assist his rook, attack the pawns left on the kingside.
>
> **(5)** Sacrifice the a-pawn to capture Black's king-side pawns.
>
> **(6)** Queen a pawn on the king-side.

Let's watch while Alekhine puts the plan into practice.

| 1 | ... | Rf6-a6 |

Blocking the pawn. Black would be forced to this position next turn anyway.

| 2 | Rd4-a4 |

Puts the rook in the right place. 2 Rd4-d5 would also win, but with more effort. Part one of the plan is complete.

| 2 | ... | Kg7-f6 |

Black's king emerges to contest the center of the board.

| 3 | Kg2-f3 | Kf6-e5 |

Black's king reaches the center first.

4   Kf3-e3

White has also centralized, so part two of his plan is complete. Will he be able to penetrate on one side of the board or the other, or will Black's king somehow be able to oppose him? That's the question for the next phase of the game.

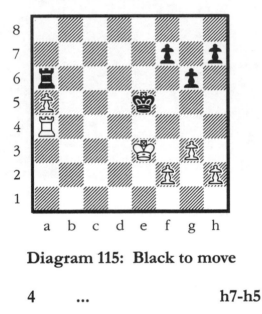

Diagram 115: Black to move

4   ...   h7-h5

Black really doesn't want to move his king-side pawns. The more he moves them, the closer they get to White's king and the easier they become to attack. Unfortunately, Black doesn't have a lot of choice.

If Black moves his rook (4 ... Ra6-a7), White just pushes his pawn closer to queening with 5 a5-a6.

If Black moves his king to the left, 4 ... Ke5-d5, White sidesteps to the right (5 Ke3-f4) to penetrate the king's-side.

If Black moves his king to the right, 4 ... Ke5-f5, White sidesteps to the left (5 Ke3-d4) and goes after the Black rook.

So Black's best chance is to leave his pieces in their current, optimal positions and try to fiddle with his pawns hoping that the weaknesses he creates won't be too damaging.

5	Ke3-d3

Alekhine threatens to move on the rook with K-c4-b5.

5	...	Ke5-d5

Black blocks that plan and keeps the kings opposed. Can he maintain the blockade?

6	Kd3-c3

Again White tries to sidestep.

6	...	Kd5-c5

And again Black takes up a blockading position.

7	Ra4-a2!

This is what's called a tempo move. White simply makes a meaningless move with his rook to throw the onus of moving onto Black. As we saw before, Black's rook can't move without letting the pawn advance, while a king move to either side allows White to penetrate on the other side.

7	...	Kc5-b5

Black sees that his best chance is to try to eliminate the pawn.

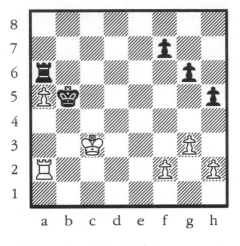

Diagram 116: White on move

8   Kc3-d4!

White sidesteps to the right and heads for the kingside. He can't protect his pawn anymore and he doesn't have to.

What both players now see is that if Black takes the White pawn, his king will be left too far out of play to stop White's attack on the king-side. After 8 ... Ra6xa5 9 Ra2xa5 check Kb5xa5, White just plays 10 Kd4-e5, followed by moving the king to f6 and capturing the pawn on f7. After that, it's just a matter of queening one of his own pawns.

8   ...   Ra6-d6 check!

Black puts up a good fight. His plan is to move the rook away with check, then push his king into a6. That way his king will stop the pawn while his rook guards the king-side. It's a clever idea, one that just might work.

9   Kd4-e5   Rd6-e6 check

Black checks again from a square where the rook is guarded. He'll move the king into a6 next turn.

10   Ke5-f4

White is still planning to attack the king-side with his king.

10   ...   Kb5-a6

Black has successfully switched defenders. Now he has to wait and see what White tries next.

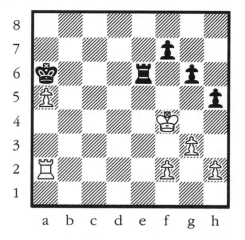

Diagram 117: White on move

11   Kf4-g5

The penetration starts. White is headed for g7 via h6.

11   ...   Re6-e5 check

Black can't stop White from reaching g7; he must try to set up a defensive formation once White's there. This check helps him reposition his rook at f5. From there, he can safely guard his f7

207

pawn, the critical weak link in his pawn chain. (The other pawns are all guarded by pawns, so they're safe.)

12	Kg5-h6	Re5-f5
13	f2-f4	

Now White threatens 14 h2-h4 followed by 15 Kh6-g7, after which Black will be completely out of playable moves.

13	...	Rf5-d5!

Black repositions the rook to guard the f7-pawn from d7. That way, the rook will have different squares to move to while still defending the pawn.

14	Kh6-g7	Rd5-d7

Can Black hold this new defensive position?

15	Kg7-f6	Rd7-c7

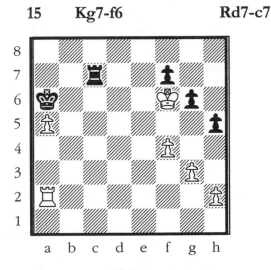

Diagram 118: White on move

Is White stymied, or is there a new way to break through?

16	f4-f5!

The pawn leads the way. This move breaks up Black's pawn chain and makes the h-pawn easier to attack.

16	...	g6xf5

Allowing White to capture on g6 isn't an improvement. If Black tries 16 ... Rc7-c6 check 17 Kf6xf7 g6xf5, White wins the king-side pawns with 18 Ra2-f2!

17	Kf6xf5

Now the pawn on h5 is vulnerable to attack.

17	...	Rc7-c5 check
18	Kf5-f6	Rc5-c7

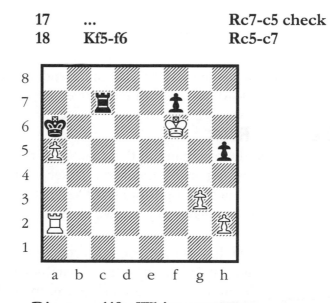

Diagram 119: White on move

19	Ra2-f2!

This is the key idea. White abandons the a-pawn, which has done its job by distracting the Black pieces, and concentrates all his firepower on the king-side pawns.

| 19 | ... | Ka6xa5 |

Black has nothing better.

| 20 | Rf2-f5 check | Ka5-b6 |
| 21 | Rf5xh5 | Kb6-c6 |

Black's king heads for the king-side as fast as possible...

| 22 | Rh5-h7 |

... but it's too late. White wins the f7-pawn as well.

| 22 | ... | Kc6-d6 |
| 23 | Rh7xf7 | |

With two extra pawns, White will win the ending pretty easily although it will still take a few more moves.

The Active Rook

As we said at the beginning of this chapter, in rook and pawn endings the most important principle is to keep your pieces active. In many, if not most positions, active, well-placed pieces are more important than being a pawn ahead.

The next position shows this principle in action. The player of the Black pieces, the great endgame artist Akiba Rubinstein, passes up many opportunities to win a quick pawn, trying instead to see that his rook and king remain actively placed. Eventually, when he feels he has a secure grip on the position, he carefully harvests his opponent's weak pawns.

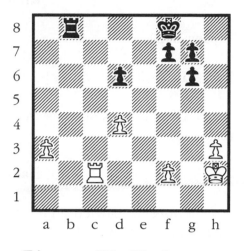

Diagram 120: Black on move

At first glance, White might appear to be doing well in Position 27. He has an outside passed pawn, on the a-file, and his rook can get behind the pawn, on the a2-square, and push it up the board.

In fact, if Black tries to win a pawn right away, he could easily get into trouble. Suppose he plays 1 ... Rb8-b3 (attacking the a-pawn) 2 Rc2-a2 Rb3-d3 (winning the d-pawn). White would ignore the attack on the d-pawn and just start pushing his passed pawn: 3 a3-a4! Rd3xd4 4 a4-a5 Rd4-c4 (to try to block the passed pawn) 5 a5-a6! Rc4-c8 6 a6-a7 Rc8-a8. Black would then be completely tied down, and White certainly wouldn't lose the position.

In rook and pawn endings, a good player avoids variations where his pieces become passive defenders. The winning idea is to make your own pieces active, while your opponent's pieces become passive. Rubinstein probably didn't spend more than a few seconds discarding the previous variation. Let's see how he decided to handle the game.

1   ...   Rb8-a8!

Black attacks the pawn at a3.

2   Rc2-c3

White protects the pawn and keeps his rook free to maneuver along the third rank.

2   ...   Ra8-a4!

Very good. Rubinstein stops the pawn dead in its tracks, while simultaneously attacking the pawn on d4.

Notice that this simple maneuver (R-a8-a4) has already given Black an active and aggressive rook, while White's rook is stuck in a defensive role guarding the a-pawn.

3   Rc3-d3

The rook guards the d-pawn, but already White is in trouble. His rook is guarding pawns, Black's rook is attacking them.

3   ...   Kf8-e7

Black's next job is to relocate the king to its best square, in this case, d5, where it attacks the pawn on d4 and threatens to penetrate the White position at either c4 or e4.

4   Kh2-g3

White tries to centralize his king as well.

4   ...   Ke7-e6
5   Kg3-f3   Ke6-d5

Black reaches the center first. Now White has to worry about losing his d-pawn at some point.

6   Kf3-e2!

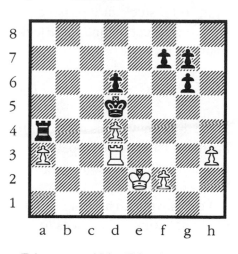

Diagram 121: Black on move

White gets to make good moves too! In this case White sets a subtle trap. Apparently Black can now just capture the pawn on d4 leaving himself a pawn ahead, but that's actually a bad mistake. If Black plays 6 ... Ra4xd4, White responds with 7 Ke2-e3! Rd4xd3 check 8 Ke3xd3. Now White will use his passed pawn on the a-file as a decoy forcing the Black king over to the edge of the board to stop it. Meanwhile the White king will move up the d-file capturing the pawn at d6 and then moving among the Black pawns on the kingside. Black might save a draw, but it would be very difficult.

Rubinstein sees through this trap. Instead of taking the bait, he improves his position, gradually depriving White of moves.

6   ...   g6-g5!

Now the White pawn at h3 can't move.

7   Rd3-b3

White doesn't want to be stuck in a passive position forever. The idea of this move is to get behind the Black pawns, trying to exchange as many as possible.

7   ...   f7-f6!

If Black captured the d-pawn with his rook, White would play 8 Rb3-d3! and again the outside passed a-pawn would give White a strong game after the rooks get exchanged.

If Black captures the d-pawn with his king, White plays Rb3-b7, and he'll pick off enough king-side pawns to get a draw.

Instead Black puts his king-side pawns on easily defendable squares. Here's what could happen if White goes after them: 8 Rb3-b7 Ra4xa3 9 Rb7xg7 Ra3xh3. Black will eventually win the d-pawn as well, leaving him two pawns ahead.

8   Ke2-e3

White now realizes his plan won't work. He settles down to a defensive position. His problem is that his pawns are isolated. They must all be defended by pieces – a cumbersome task.

8   ...   Kd5-c4

Black keeps grabbing more space. The more active your pieces are, the more space they can eventually control.

9   Rb3-d3

The only square for the rook if White doesn't want to lose his a-pawn and h-pawn. But now White's pieces are starting to run out of squares. The rook has no moves, and the king has to stay where it protects the rook.

9   ...   d6-d5!

Takes the square e4 away from the White king.

10   Ke3-d2

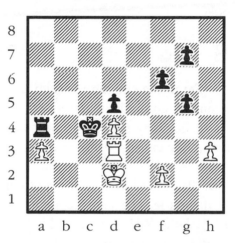

Diagram 122: Black on move

10   ...   Ra4-a8!

An excellent repositioning move. The rook has done its job at a4. Now that Black's king controls the queenside, the rook seeks more activity. Black's main idea is to invade along the b-file, as in this variation: 11 Kd2-e3 Ra8-b8 12 Ke3-d2 Rb8-b2 check 13 Kd2-e3 Rb2-a2. White is almost out of moves.

11   Kd2-c2

Temporarily stops that idea.

11	...	Ra8-a7!

Black waits until White moves his king back to d2.

12	Kc2-d2

White can't move his rook anywhere without losing either the d-pawn or the a-pawn, and this is the only square where the king can guard the rook.

12	...	Ra7-e7!

This move puts White into a situation known as zugswang – a German word meaning "compulsion to move." If White didn't have to move, he'd be okay (Black doesn't actually have a threat). Any actual move causes White to lose in some way.

If White keeps shuffling his king, he'll eventually lose his a-pawn, and with it the game. The sequence would be 13 Kd2-c2 Re7-e2 check 14 Rd3-d2 Re2xd2 check 15 Kc2xd2 Kc4-b3! followed by capturing the a-pawn. The resulting ending with just kings and pawns would be a win for Black.

13	Rd3-c3 check

White realizes he can't hold on to everything, so he abandons the d-pawn to get some activity for his rook.

13	...	Kc4xd4

Black records his first profit for his fine maneuvering.

14	a3-a4!

White uses his best asset, the passed a-pawn. With his rook behind it on a3, this could become a powerful force.

| 14 | ... | Re7-a7 |
| 15 | Rc3-a3 | Ra7-a5! |

Black blockades the pawn as quickly as possible.

| 16 | Ra3-a1 |

Although White has a passed pawn, there's no way to advance it, so he begins shuttling his rook between a3 and a1.

16	...	Kd4-c4
17	Kd2-e3	d5-d4 check
18	Ke3-d2	

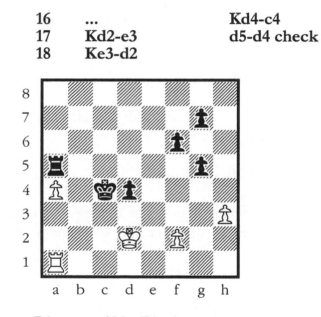

Diagram 123: Black on move

Black's made as much progress as he can with the current arrangement of pieces. In these endings, when your opponent has managed to block your progress, the way to move forward is to open up a new front.

18	...	Ra5-f5!

The right idea. Black goes after the weak f-pawn, which White left undefended when he tried to block Black's progress on the queenside. Black has calculated exactly – he'll be able to pick off the f-pawn and get back in time to stop the a-pawn.

19	Kd2-e1

An abject retreat, but White saw that Black had calculated correctly. If White pushed his a-pawn, this is what would have happened: 19 a4-a5 Rf5xf2 check 20 Kd2-e1 Rf2-b2 21 a5-a6 Rb2-b8 22 a6-a7 Rb8-a8, arriving just in time. Black would then move his king back, Kc4-c5-b6, and capture the a-pawn with his rook.

19	...	Kc4-b4

Just as we saw in the previous ending: Black is switching blockaders, to free his rook to attack the f-pawn and h-pawn.

20	Ke1-e2	Kb4-a4

The pawn is securely blocked and the rook is free. If White's rook ever leaves the a-file, the king will capture the pawn.

21	Ra1-a3	Rf5-f4

A good square for the rook. It guards the d-pawn while still attacking the White pawns.

22	Ra3-a2

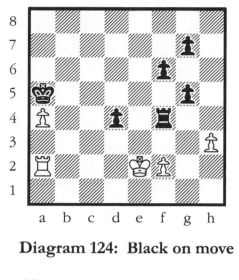

Diagram 124: Black on move

22	...	Rf4-h4!

Black goes after the h-pawn. If White tries to defend it with 23 Ra2-a3, Black plays 23 ... Ka5-b4! and the rook can no longer defend both the a-pawn and the h-pawn. That's an example of the tactical theme called "The Overworked Piece," which I explained in detail in my other chess books with Cardoza Publishing.

23	Ke2-d3	Rh4xh3 check
24	Kd3xd4	Rh3-h4 check!

Another tactical theme, this time the Skewer. Black checks the king and wins the a-pawn, located behind the king on the same line.

25	Kd4-d3	Rh4xa4

Black is now two pawns ahead, and White's king is cut off from the Black pawns. From this point on, the win is pretty easy.

26   Ra2-e2

If White exchanges rooks he has no chance. From e2, the rook is hoping to reach e7 or e8, where it may cause some trouble among the Black pawns.

26   ...   Ra4-f4!

Ties the White rook down to guarding the f-pawn.

27   Kd3-e3

The king takes over the job of guarding the f-pawn, freeing the rook for further action. Although White should lose this ending now, he's still going to try to put up stiff resistance. A tactical trick or two may well appear, and if Black relaxes his attention, White might still save the game.

27   ...   Ka5-b6

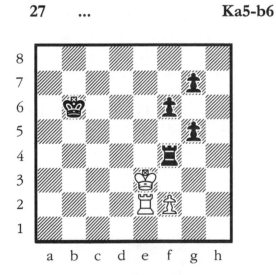

Diagram 125: White on move

28   Re2-c2!

White keeps fighting. This move cuts the Black king off from the king-side.

28	...	Kb6-b7

The White rook could become a nuisance if White were allowed to play Rc2-c8-g8, getting behind the Black pawns. The king move keeps the rook out.

29	Rc2-c1

White temporizes, waiting for Black to try something. The upside to White's losing his pawns is that his pieces don't have much to protect anymore. They're free to roam around.

29	...	Rf4-a4

The rook can't do much from f4. One idea is to move it to c8 via a8, enabling the king to cross over to the kingside.

30	Rc1-h1

Threatening to win a pawn by Rh1-h7 and Rxg7.

30	...	Kb7-c6

Opens up the seventh rank. Black can now respond to Rh1-h7 with Ra4-a7.

31	Rh1-h7	Ra4-a7
32	Ke3-e4	Kc6-d6

The king will take over the job of defending the pawns.

33	Ke4-f5

White overlooks a tactical shot which finishes the game. If White had stayed back with his king, Black would still have won by advancing his pawns, but it would have been a slow process.

33	...	g7-g6 check!

Attacks the king and uncovers an attack on the rook.

34	Kf5xg6	Ra7xh7
35	Kg6xh7	Kd6-e5!

The Black king moves in on the last White pawn. The White king is caught offside.

36	Kh7-g6	g5-g4!

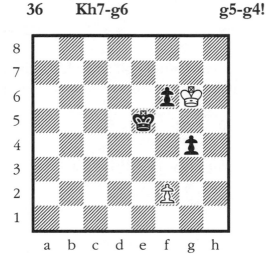

Diagram 126: White resigns

White can't stop Black from eventually queening a pawn.

QUEEN AGAINST PAWN

Queen against pawn? Doesn't that sound like a pretty big mismatch? What chance can a lowly pawn have against a powerful queen? In most cases, not much. But in a few cases, the side with the pawn can actually fight the mighty queen to a draw.

FIRST WORD
Even a pawn can have a chance against a queen. In this chapter you'll learn how.

Let's look at how, and perhaps you'll be able to pull out an amazing save in one of your own games!

Winning Against a Too-Far-Back Pawn

Diagram 127: White on move

223

The first point to notice about these endings is that unless the pawn has advanced to its seventh rank, one square away from queening) it doesn't have much of a chance. Diagram 127 shows why. Although White's king and queen couldn't be farther away, and the pawn is already on its sixth row, White stops it easily.

1	Qh8-h1!	a3-a2
2	Qh1-a1!	

That's it. Once the queen gets in front of the pawn, she just sits there until White brings up the king, and then White's two pieces will force Black's king away from the pawn.

2	...	Kb4-b3
3	Kg7-f6	Kb3-a3

To avoid losing the pawn, Black's king has to shuttle between b3 and a3. Meanwhile White closes in for the kill.

4	Kf6-e5	Ka3-b3
5	Ke5-d4	Kb3-a3
6	Kd4-c4!	

The quickest finish.

6	...	Ka3-a4
7	Qa1xa2 checkmate	

If the pawn is already on the seventh rank, ready to queen, the other side has more problems.

Take a look at the next position.

Winning Against a Center Pawn

Diagram 128: White on move

White can still win here, but it's not as easy as in the last example. First he has to gain time for his king to approach.

1	Qg8-c4 check	Kc2-b2

Black threatens to queen the pawn again.

2	Qc4-d3!

White attacks the pawn and also prevents queening.

2	...	Kb2-c1

Black guards the pawn and again threatens to queen.

3	Qd3-c3 check!

This is the key move. To save his pawn, Black has to block it with his king.

225

| 3 | ... | Kc1-d1 |
| 4 | Kg6-f5 | |

When the pawn is blocked, White uses the time to bring his king closer.

| 4 | ... | Kd1-e2 |

Black emerges on the other side and again threatens to queen.

| 5 | Qc3-c2! | |

Now White pins the pawn against the king.

| 5 | ... | Ke2-e1 |

The only move to save the pawn.

| 6 | Qc2-e4 check | |

White executes the same maneuver as before to push the Black king in front of the pawn.

6	...	Ke1-f2
7	Qe4-d3	Kf2-e1
8	Qd3-e3 check	Ke1-d1
9	Kf5-e4	

White closes in.

9	...	Kd1-c2
10	Qe3-d3 check	Kc2-c1
11	Qd3-c3 check	Kc1-d1

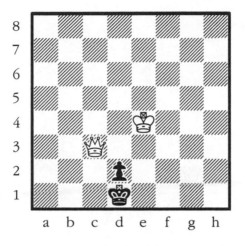

Diagram 129: White on move

With White's king closing in, he has a checkmate in three moves.

12	Ke4-e3	Kd1-e1
13	Qc3xd2 check	Ke1-f1
14	Qd2-f2 checkmate	

Drawing Against a Bishop's Pawn

Does this line of play mean that you can always win against a pawn on the seventh rank? Surprisingly the answer is no. The method you've just learned works perfectly well if the pawn is on the king file (e-file), the queen file (d-file), or either knight file (b-file or g-file).

But if the pawn is on one of the bishop's files (c-file or f-file), it won't work if the defender knows a tactical trick!

Take a look at the next position.

Diagram 130: White on move

This is the same as Position 128, but all the pieces have moved one file to the left. Now the Black pawn is on the c-file, and this means Black can draw the game if he knows how. Let's watch how the play develops.

1   **Qf8-b4 check**

White starts as before. He wants to push the Black king in front of the pawn so his own king can approach.

1	...	Kb2-a2
2	Qb4-c3	Ka2-b1
3	Qc3-b3 check	

Diagram 131: Black on move

So far so good. Now White expects the Black king to move to c1, and he'll use the next move to bring his own king closer. But look what Black has in mind.

3 ... Kb1-a1!

Black doesn't protect the pawn at all! He just sticks his king in the corner, and if White plays 4 Qb3xc2, it's a stalemate!

White is stuck. He has to keep checking, and can't ever gain a move to bring up his king. The game is a draw.

The side with the pawn isn't the only side with tactical tricks in these endings. If White's king is close enough to the scene of the action, he can win against a bishop pawn, provided his queen is also in the right place. Take a look at the next diagram.

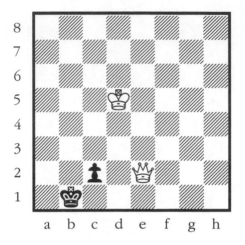

Diagram 132: White to move can force a win

Black threatens to queen his pawn. White's response: go ahead!

> **1   Kd5-c4!**

White actually allows Black to queen with check!

> **1   ...   c2-c1 (Q) check**

"It's a draw now," thinks Black.

> **2   Kc4-b3!**

Suddenly Black is short of moves. White's threat is Qe2-a2 checkmate. If Black checks on b2 or c2, White's queen captures. If Black moves his queen anywhere else, White plays Qe2-b2 checkmate. Black got his queen, but he couldn't stop checkmate. If Black has a rook's pawn (a-file or h-file) on the seventh rank against a queen, that's also a draw. When White maneuvers to force the Black king in front of the pawn, Black is stalemated. Again, White won't have time to advance his own king.

QUEEN & PAWN AGAINST QUEEN

Endings where a queen and pawn try to defeat a lone queen are especially tricky, and cause problems for even the best players. The defender has plenty of chances to draw the game, with a powerful queen roaming the board and ready to give check at every turn.

FIRST WORD
Even the best players have difficulty defeating a lone queen with just a queen and a pawn.

There are a few simple rules, however, which will allow you to play these endings pretty well. If you know them, you'll be way ahead of your opponents, and you'll be able to save many a lost game, or turn a theoretically drawn game into a win.

Defender in Front of the Pawn

The first rule is an easy one, very similar to the situation in rook endings. If the defender's king can block the pawn, the game should be a draw.

Take a look at Position 133:

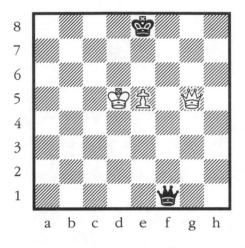

Diagram 133: Black on move

White has a pawn on the e-file, but Black has managed to get his king to e8, a square in front of the pawn. Now Black can draw the game pretty simply, just by checking with his queen. Here's how the play might go.

| 1 | ... | Qf1-b5 check |

Black's plan is just to annoy the king with a lot of checks. Sometimes he can even set a trap or two.

| 2 | Kd5-e4 |

Did you see the trap? If White played the apparently aggressive 2 Kd5-e6??, Black could checkmate him in two moves! 2 ... Qb5-d7 check 3 Ke6-f6 (forced) Qd7-f7 checkmate! The queen can be a very powerful defender indeed!

| 2 | ... | Qb5-c4 check |
| 3 | Ke4-f5 |

Black had another trap: if White played 3 Ke4-e3, Black would play Qc4-c1 check!, winning the White queen with a skewer.

| 3 | ... | Qc4-d3 check |

Another trap: if White plays 4 Kf5-e6, Black again checkmates after 4 ... Qd3-d7.

| 4 | Kf5-f6 |

White is trying to get away from the checks.

| 4 | ... | Qd3-d8 check! |

This is the simplest way to draw. Black aims to exchange queens and then draw the pawn ending.

5	Kf6-g6	Qd8xg5 check
6	Kg6xg5	Ke8-e7!
7	Kg5-f5	Ke7-f7!

If you remember your king and pawn endings from earlier in the book, you know that this endgame is a draw.

Winning with a Blocking Check

To have real winning chances in these endings, White (the side with the extra pawn) needs to get his pawn to the seventh rank. Where should Black's king be if he can't get right in front of the pawn? Amazingly, if the Black king can't actually block the pawn, he should get as far away from the pawn as possible! This is completely different from the situation in all other endings where the defending king is always trying to get as close to the passed pawns as possible.

The reason the defender's king wants to get far away is that the defender's best chances lie in creating a perpetual check with his queen. For this to work, the defender's queen needs to have freedom of movement around the pawn. If the king is close by, it may well get in the way.

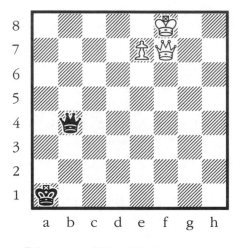

Diagram 134: White on move

Diagram 134 shows a pretty easy win for White. Right now Black's queen is pinning the pawn to White's king. Black's king is far away, but unfortunately it's located on a bad diagonal. Watch what happens:

> 1   Kf8-g8

Unpinning the pawn, threatening 2 e7-e8 (Q). Black has to check somewhere. But if he checks on the first rank (Qb4-b8 check), White wins by pushing his pawn. That only leaves Black a single check.

> 1   ...   Qb4-g4 check
> 2   Qf7-g7 check!

This is the standard winning idea. White tries to maneuver so he can block a check with a check, thus trading off queens.

2	...	Qg4xg7 check
3	Kg8xg7	

...and White queens his pawn next turn.

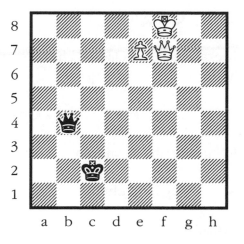

Diagram 135: White on move

In Position 135, Black's king is on a different square, c2. White can still win, but it requires slightly more time.

1	Kf8-g8

The first step is to unpin the pawn and threaten to advance.

1	...	Qb4-g4 check

Black can't stop the pawn. He distracts White with a check.

2	Kg8-h8

Again threatening to push the pawn.

2　...　Qg4-d4 check

Black can't check on h4 or h3 because White plays Qf7-h7 check! (again blocking a check with a check) and the queens come off the board with an easy win for White.

3　Qf7-g7!

Stopping the checks, since 3 ... Qd4-h4 check is still answered by 4 Qg7-h7 check.

3　...　Qd4-d7

The only way left to stop the pawn from queening.

4　Qg7-g6 check!

Once again the Black king is caught on an awkward diagonal. The White queen checks and guards e8, the queening square. Next turn White will play e7-e8(Q), winning.

Defeating a Well-Placed King

If the Black king is on a good defensive square, White may not have such an easy win at his disposal. White's best winning try in this case is to centralize his queen, then bring his king toward Black's king.

Lining his king up with Black's king will create more winning checks. Look at the next position.

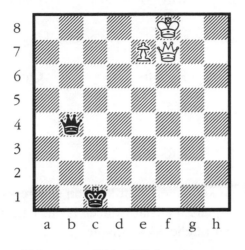

Diagram 136: White on move

The c1 square is a great defensive square for Black's king. In the last two positions, Black's trouble came when the White queen blocked a check on either g7 or h7. The bad squares for Black's king are squares in the lower corner of the board which are on the diagonals leading to either g7 or h7 — squares like a1, b2, c3, b1, and c2. By avoiding those squares, Black forces White to find a new winning idea.

> **1   Qf7-d5**

Escaping with the king into the corner won't work in this position, as Black will just keep checking and White won't be able to block with a check. So White first centralizes his queen (cutting down on Black's checking squares), and then prepares to move his king out.

> **1   ...   Qb4-f4 check**

Black keeps checking, as usual.

2	Kf8-g7	Qf4-c7

Pinning the pawn is just as effective as checking.

3	Kg7-f6	Qc7-b6 check

The checks continue.

4	Kf6-f5	

In general, it's good to keep your king on squares of the oppo-site color of the square the Black queen is on. This will slightly reduce the number of checks available.

4	...	Qb6-f2 check

Black only had two checks available (f2 and b1). The f2 check gives him the most options next turn.

5	Kf5-e6	

White heads for the d, c, and b-files, where he'll have more pos-sibilities of blocking checks with checks. Since Black's queen is now on a dark square, White stays on white squares.

5	...	Qf2-b6 check
6	Qd5-d6	

This interposition again leaves Black with just two checks (b3 and e3).

6	...	Qb6-b3 check
7	Ke6-d7	

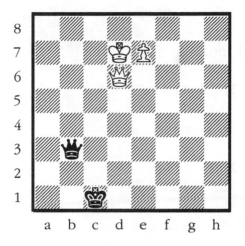

Diagram 137: Black on move

Black is running out of checks. If he plays Qb3-a4 check or b5 check, White blocks with Qd6-c6 check! (Notice the power of moving the king to the same files as Black's king.)

	7	...	Qb3-h3 check

The only check left.

	8	Kd7-d8	Qh3-h4

With no checks left, Black must pin the pawn.

	9	Qd6-d7

Covers the king.

	9	...	Qh4-g5

Black has to maintain the pin.

10	Kd8-c8	Qg5-c5 check

The only check, but now ...

11	Qd7-c7!	

This forces the exchange of queens.

11	...	Qc5xc7 check
12	Kc8xc7	

White queens his pawn next turn.

QUEEN & PAWNS AGAINST QUEEN & PAWNS

The combination of a passed pawn and an escorting queen is so powerful that even an enemy queen cannot stop the pawn by herself. Take a look at the position below.

FIRST WORD

In endings with just queens and pawns on the board, the winning idea is to be the first side to create a passed pawn.

Power of a Passed Pawn

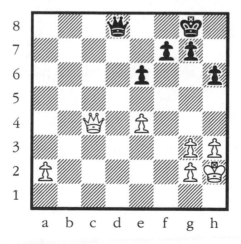

Diagram 138: White on move

White is a pawn ahead and has an outside passed pawn. If this were an ending of bishop versus bishop, knight versus knight, or rook versus rook, White's extra pawn would be enough to win, but the process would be long and slow, as we've seen in some previous games.

But with queens on the board, watch what happens.

> **1   a2-a4**

Push the pawn!

> **1   ...   Qd8-a5**

Black immediately moves to blockade. Now what?

> **2   Qc4-b5!**

This is the key idea. White's pawn supports the queen, and the queen chases the Black queen out of the way.

> **2   ...   Qa5-a7**

The queen falls back to a new blockading square.

> **3   a4-a5**

Push the pawn!

> **3   ...   Kg8-h7**
> **4   a5-a6!**

Keep pushing!

> **4   ...   g7-g5**

There's not a lot that Black can do.

>5   Qb5-b7!

Once more the queen sweeps Black out of the way.

>5   ...   Qa7-d4

Black has to move or be captured.

>6   a6-a7!

Swift and brutal. White gets a second queen next turn.

In Diagram 138, Black simply had no chance. Accompanied by its queen, the pawn could just race to the queening square almost as quickly as if there were no pieces on the board.

Defending Against a Passed Pawn

There are only two defenses to a passed pawn in a queen ending:

(1) Another passed pawn. If both sides have passed pawns, the side whose pawn is further advanced has the advantage. It may be worth sacrificing a pawn or two just to get a passed pawn loose.

(2) Perpetual check. In the last diagram, White's king had a cozy little nest, so there was nothing Black could do. If the king's position isn't as secure, the defender may be able to organize a perpetual check.

Now let's look at some more difficult endings, where the defender has a chance of putting up a fight.

In Position 139, Black is a pawn down and White's king is very aggressively placed, but Black has a powerful passed pawn on the a-file. With good play, this is enough to win. Let's watch.

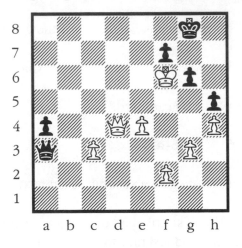

Diagram 139: Black on move

Black's first job is to stop the threat of 1 Qd4-d8 check and 2 Kf6xf7, with mating threats.

1   ...   Qa3-f8!

A fine move which accomplishes several goals in one stroke. It prevents Q-d8 check, it guards Black's king, it clears the way for the a-pawn to advance, and it indirectly guards the a-pawn itself. Do you see what happens if White now plays 2 Qd4xa4?

2   Kf6-g5

White prudently decides to retreat his king out of the danger zone. He sees that if he carelessly played 2 Qd4xa4??, Black would reply 2 ... Qf8-d6 check, and after 3 Kf6-g5 Kg8-g7! Black would have unstoppable threats of Qd6-e5 checkmate and f7-f6 checkmate.

2	...	Qf8-e7 check!

Chases the White king a little farther back while moving the queen to a more active square.

3	Kg5-f4	a4-a3

Black has a simple plan — queen the a-pawn. White must stop the pawn, since there's no way his own pawns can be mobilized fast enough.

4	Kf4-e3

The king is the slow-moving piece, so it has to get mobilized first. After 4 Qd4-a4 Qe7-c5! the White king might not be able to reach the queenside.

4	...	Qe7-b7

Prepares to go to b3 or b2 to help the pawn advance.

5	Qd4-d8 check

White has to stop the pawn as soon as possible. This check is part of a relocating maneuver that brings the queen to a5 via d8.

5	...	Kg8-h7!

The right square for the king. On g7, the king would be subject to annoying checks along the d4-h8 diagonal. On h7, the only way White could give a check would be to somehow capture the f7 pawn. (Black will be very careful to see that doesn't happen.) Remember that the defender's best chance to draw is to somehow give perpetual check, so shielding your king from check is a top priority for the side trying to win.

> 6   Qd8-a5

Stops the pawn for the moment.

> 6   ...   Qb7-b2

The threat couldn't be plainer: a3-a2-a1 (Q).

> 7   Qa5-c7

A counter-threat: White wants to play Qc7xf7 check, followed by a perpetual check on f7 and f8.

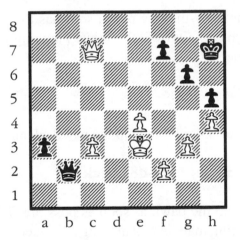

Diagram 140: Black on move

> 7   ...   Qb2-b3!

Black puts a stop to that nonsense. From b3 the queen guards the key f7-square and also helps the pawn advance. In addition, it pins the c-pawn, so White can't play c3-c4, cutting off the queen's protection of f7.

> 8   g2-g4

White is getting desperate. To give check, he has to somehow blast open the alleys leading to the Black king. This pawn sacrifice may help. If Black plays 8 ... h5xg4, White will try 9 h4-h5!, opening up some lines of attack.

| 8 | ... | a3-a2 |

Black doesn't fall for the bait, but pushes resolutely on toward a1.

| 9 | Qc7-a5 | |

Stops the pawn for the moment.

| 9 | ... | Qb3-b2 |

Again prepares to push the pawn to a1. Can White manufacture a perpetual check?

| 10 | Qa5-c7 | Kh7-g8! |

A clever idea. Black allows White to check, for the purpose of maneuvering his queen to a bad square.

| 11 | Qc7-d8 check | Kg8-g7 |
| 12 | Qd8-d4 check | Kg7-h7 |

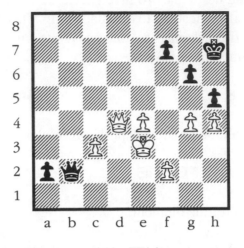

Diagram 141: White on move

White's queen is now at d4; it can't return to c7. That particular square is crucial because it's the only square where the White queen performs three (!) crucial tasks: attacks f7, guards c3, and prevents the Black queen from returning to the seventh rank herself.

13   Qd4-c4

White does what he can. From this square the queen threatens f7 again and still guards c3. But White has no control over the seventh rank any longer, so watch what happens.

13   ...   Qb2-b6 check

The Black queen relocates with check.

14   Ke3-e2   Qb6-a7!

The square Black wanted to reach. The queen gets behind the pawn and guards f7 as well. Now the pawn can't be stopped.

15	g4xh5

White opens up the kingside, but to no avail.

15	...	a2-a1(Q)
16	h5xg6 check	f7xg6

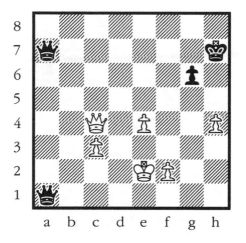

Diagram 142: White resigns

White has no checks, and the two queens together on an open board overwhelm him. A typical finish might be 17 h4-h5 Qa1-b2 check, and now White gets checkmated very quickly:

If 18 Ke2-d1 or e1 Qa7-a1 checkmate.

If 18 Ke2-f1 Q (either one)xf2 checkmate.

If 18 Ke2-d3 Qa7-d7 check 19 Kd3-e3 Qb2-d2 check 20 Ke3-f3 Qd7-h3 checkmate.

If 18 Ke2-f3 Qb2xf2 check 19 Kf3-g4 Qa7-d7 check with a quick mate to follow.

Creating Checkmating Chances

If you know how to handle the queen properly, there are winning chances in queen endings that don't exist in other endings, because the queen can be a powerful checkmating force all by herself. Take a look at Diagram 143:

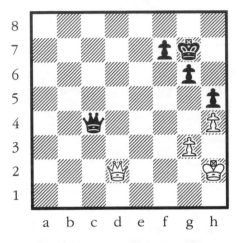

Diagram 143: Black on move

Black is a pawn ahead, but all the pawns are on one side of the board. If we replaced the two queen with two rooks, or two bishops, the ending would be a pretty simple draw for White. He would exchange pawns when possible, and eventually he'd block the last pawn with his king. Black then wouldn't be able to make progress.

With queens on the board, Black concocts a different plan. He's going to boldly march his king right into the heart of enemy territory (he's headed for the f1 square!) and try to either checkmate White or force an exchange of queens. Can White stop this simple idea? We'll see.

By the way, here's another handy rule of thumb for queen endings: verify that the ending with the queens off the board is a win for you. If it is, you can make progress by offering (or threatening) to exchange queens. Your opponent will have to back down each time, and allow you to carry out your plan. You'll see Black use this approach a few times in this ending.

1	...	Kg7-f6

Black's queen is already very well-placed. It controls many center squares (cutting down on White's checks) and guards the key pawn at f7. So Black starts the king out on his march.

2	Qd2-d8 check

White can't improve his king's position, so he starts a series of checks.

2	...	Kf6-f5

Black boldly heads for White's territory.

3	Qd8-d7 check

White will continue checking as long as he can. Black has to demonstrate that, at some point, he can avoid the checks.

3	...	Kf5-e4
4	Qd7-e7 check	

Because the Black queen controls the board, White actually only had two checks left, e7 and b7. From b7 he wouldn't be able to get back and give a check at b3, so he chooses e7.

4	...	Ke4-d3
5	Qe7-d7 check	Kd3-e2

Black has just about completed the first step of his plan. His king is closing in on the White king.

6   Qd7-e7 check   Qc4-e6

This move blocks any checks. Notice that with the White queen on a dark square, and the Black king on a white square, the queen can't move along a diagonal and give a check. That's an important motif for cutting down on checks in the ending.

7   Qe7-b7

The queen heads for g2, to start checking again.

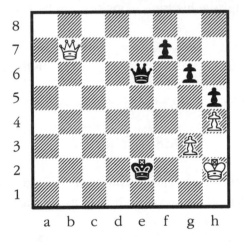

Diagram 144: Black on move

7   ...   f7-f5!

A good move, creating a square for the queen at e4. Under some circumstances, the pawn may push on to f4, breaking up the White king's defenses.

8   Qb7-g2 check

252

White starts a new series of checks from g2.

Depending on the pawn structure, the queen may not be especially effective checking the king from close range. The king will himself control many of the queen's checking squares, so the queen will always have to be located at least two squares away, and if the pawns get in the way, there may not be a lot of checking squares at that distance.

8	...	Ke2-e3

Now, for example, White has only one available check, at g1.

9	Qg2-b2

White moves the queen over to the open queenside, where there's more room for checks.

If White tries to stick close to the kingside, he can quickly be maneuvered out of checking room. Here's a typical sequence: 9 Qg2-g1 check Ke3-e2 10 Qg1-g2 check Ke2-d3 11 Qg2-f3 check Kd2-d2 12 Qf3-f4 check Kd2-e2! and White has no more checks. The spaces on the queenside offer better prospects.

9	...	Qe6-c4

The Black queen gets back to the center while controlling a bunch of key checking squares.

10	Qb2-a3 check	Qc4-d3

Blocks the check while setting a new trap. If White plays 11 Qa3-c1 check, Black answers with Qd3-d2 check, forcing off the queens.

11	Qa3-c5 check	Ke3-f3

This leaves White only one check, on c6.

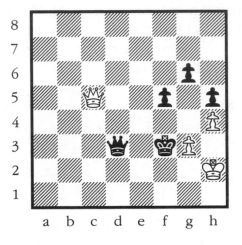

Diagram 145: White on move

12	Qc5-c6 check	Qd3-e4

This move contains another trap, thanks to the aggressive position of Black's king. If White tries to equalize material with 13 Qc6xg6, Black forces checkmate: 13 ... Qe4-e2 check 14 Kh2-g1 Qe2-g2 checkmate.

13	Qc6-c3 check

White sees through that trap and keeps checking.

13	...	Kf3-f2

Threatening Qe4-g2 checkmate.

14	Qc3-c5 check	Qe4-e3

Black blocks the check with a new threat: 15 ... Qe3xg3 check 16 Kh2-h1 Qg3-g1 checkmate.

15   Qc5-c2 check

This is the only check left.

15   ...   Qe3-e2!

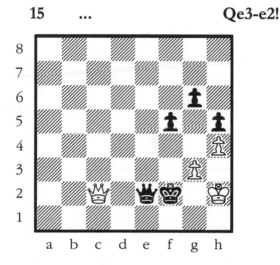

Diagram 146: White on move

The lineup of the Black queen and the White king on the same rank is the beginning of the end. If White plays 16 Qc2-c5 check, Black has 16 ... Kf2-f3 check and 17 ... Qe2-g2 checkmate.

16   Qc2-c6

The best defense, guarding g2, where most mates occur.

16   ...   Kf2-f1 check!
17   Kh2-h3

The only square. If White plays 17 Kh2-h1, Black trades queens with 17 ... Qe2-e4 check!

17	...	Kf1-g1

Closing in. Now the threats are Qe2-h2 checkmate or Qe2-g4 checkmate or Qe2-f1 check, mating next turn.

18	Qc6-c5 check

White has one last ingenious defensive try.

18	...	Qe2-f2
19	Qc5-e3!	

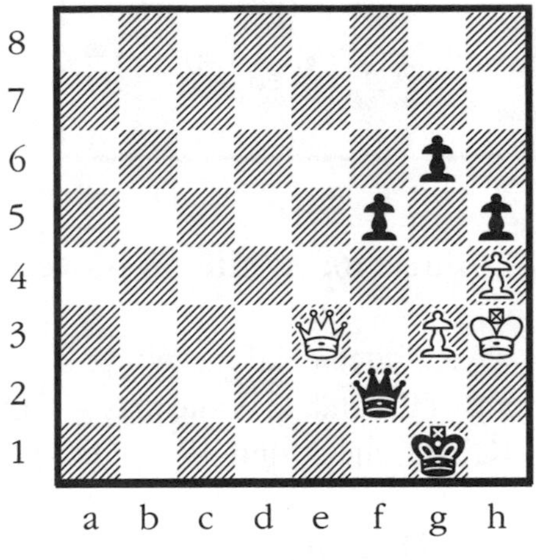

Diagram 147: Black on move

This is it! If Black grabs the queen, 19 ... Qf2xe3, White is stalemated and the game is a draw! But Black is too sharp.

19	...	f5-f4!

This finishes it. If 20 g3xf4, Black has 20 ... Qf2xe3 checkmate, or if 20 Qe3xf4 Qf2-g2 checkmate.

20	Qe3xf2 check	Kg1xf2
21	g3xf4	Kf2-f3!

Black captures the f-pawn next turn, and the h-pawn in a couple of turns. After that his own pawns queen easily.

QUEEN AGAINST TWO ROOKS

Beginners favor having the queen in this ending, since the queen is much more powerful than either rook separately, and coordinating the rooks can be a tough chore. The more experienced player understands the brutal power of two rooks in tandem, and knows that the queen can have a difficult time holding her own.

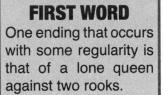

FIRST WORD
One ending that occurs with some regularity is that of a lone queen against two rooks.

Rooks on a Wide-Open Board

Our next ending shows the power of the two rooks against the queen when the board is wide open and the two rooks can cooperate against the enemy king. It's from a game in 1957 between Sammy Reshevsky (Black) and Donald Byrne (White).

Reshevsky is generally considered the second-best American player of all time, behind Bobby Fischer. He dominated American chess from the 1930s to the 1950s, when Fischer appeared on the scene, and he remained a dangerous opponent up until his retirement in the 1980s. Donald Byrne was one of the young American stars to appear in New York after World War II. His promising career was cut short by an untimely illness. His brother, Robert, still edits the chess column for the New York Times. Diagram 148 shows the position after White has played c3-c4.

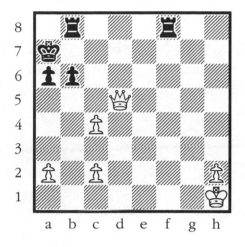

Diagram 148: Black (Reshevsky) on move

Just counting pieces and pawns in Position 148 might give you the impression that White is doing well. He has a queen and two pawns against Black's two rooks. His queen seems powerfully placed in the center of the board, while Black's rooks do not seem very influential.

But first impressions can be deceiving. Actually, White's in serious trouble. Why? Because his pawns are all isolated.

An isolated pawn is a pawn that doesn't have a friendly pawn on either adjacent file. White's a-pawn is isolated because White doesn't have a pawn on the b-file to protect it if the need arises. The two White pawns on the c-file are isolated since there are no White pawns on the b-file or d-file. Isolated pawns can't be protected by other pawns, so they have to be protected by pieces. And that's a problem if your opponent has more pieces than you do. If Black's two rooks both gang up to attack a White pawn, White's queen won't be much use in the defense. The rooks will just gobble up the pawn, then go on to attack the next one.

Actually Black has a pretty simple winning plan in Position 148. It requires these three steps:

(1) Use the rooks in tandem to capture the White c-pawns and the h-pawn, clearing the board and exposing the White king.

(2) Herd the White king to the edge of the board.

(3) Use one rook to keep the king trapped on the edge while the other rook gives checkmate.

How can White fight against this plan? He has only one weapon – to try to use the open board to give perpetual check with the queen. To avoid perpetual check, the Black king will need to stay in the corner where it currently resides, and Black's rooks will have to do double duty, guarding the approaches to the king while accomplishing the steps in Black's own plan.

Let's watch Reshevsky at work, as he shows us how to make progress methodically.

1 ... Rf8-c8

The first step is to clear away the White pawns. He'll start with the c-pawns, so he brings one rook to bear on the c-file.

2 Qd5-d7 check Ka7-a8

Unfortunately, Black can't stick a rook on b7 without losing the rook on c8. So the king has to retreat.

3 Kh1-g1

The White king doesn't want to be on the edge of the board, so White starts to move it toward the center. The longer White can keep his king in the center, the better off he'll be.

Why doesn't White guard his attacked pawn on c4? He doesn't have to! The pawn is indirectly guarded. If Black tries 3 ... Rc8xc4?? White replies with 4 Qd7-d5 check! The double attack on Black's king and rook will win the loose rook next turn.

Does White expect Black to fall into this trap? No. The point of noticing small traps like this is to save time. White doesn't waste a move guarding his c-pawn since it's already guarde. Instead, he just brings his king closer to the action. Seeing the threats and traps already in the position give you a way of using your pieces more efficently. That's part of what winning chess is all about.

3	...	Rc8-c5

The rook moves to a protected square so that the other rook can switch over to c8, piling up on the c-pawn. Black has to maneuver slowly and carefully, so that the White queen can't do any damage.

4	Kg1-f1	Rb8-c8

Now that Black has doubled rooks on the c-file, it's curtains for the front c-pawn. Even if White protects the pawn with his queen, Black will just snap it off.

5	h2-h4

White will push his h-pawn as far as he can, giving Black something else to worry about.

5	...	Rc5xc4

6	h4-h5

White can't do anything about the rear c-pawn, so he doesn't bother try. The h-pawn could cause trouble if it advances further.

6	...	Rc4xc2

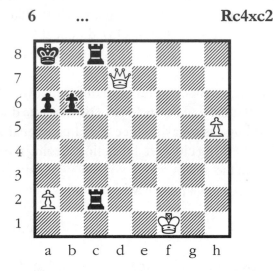

Diagram 149: White on move

The c-pawns have fallen with no resistance. Now Black turns his attention to the pesky h-pawn.

7	h5-h6	Rc8-c7

A move with two purposes. The rook on c7 guards the h7 square, preventing the White pawn from advancing further. It also forms a secure nest for Black's king. With a rook on c7 and the king on a7, Black will be safe from any annoying checks, which will allow him to turn his full attention to the h-pawn.

8	Qd7-a4

Threatens Qa4xa6 check.

8	...	Ka8-a7

Stops that threat. Now Black is ready to go after the h-pawn with his other rook.

9	Qa4-f4	Rc2-c6

The front rook attacks the pawn. Black now threatens Rc7-h7, ganging up on the poor pawn.

10	Kf1-e2

White can't do much about the threat, so he moves his king into the center.

Diagram 150: Black on move

Black could now just capture the h-pawn by playing Rc7-h7 and Rc6xh6. Instead, Black gives a series of checks, which don't really change the position, and only then captures the pawn. The reason for the series of meaningless checks is to gain time on his clock.

All tournament chess games are played with time clocks, which record the amount of time used by each player. If a player uses more than his allotted time (called overstepping the clock) he loses the game, regardless of the position on the board. A player running low on time, who sees a way to repeat a series of moves, might play those moves quickly just to improve his time situation. There's nothing unethical about such a maneuver, and if you watch a tournament you'll see that situation come up a few times.

10	...	Rc7-e7 check
11	Ke2-d3	Re7-d7 check
12	Kd3-e3	Rc6-e6 check
13	Ke3-f3	Rd7-h7

Back to the main plan.

| 14 | Qf4-f8 | Re6xh6 |

Diagram 151: White on move

It would have been a mistake to capture with the other rook. If Black had played 14 ... Rh7xh6, the seventh rank would have been left unguarded, and White would have replied with 15

264

Qf8-f7 check, followed by a series of checks on f8 and f7. The only way for Black to escape these checks would be to bring his king out into the open via c6, but that would open up still more checking possibilities on the wide-open board. To have a hope of winning, Black has to keep his king sheltered from checks, which in turn means keeping the seventh row guarded by a rook.

Black's next step is to try to herd the White king to the edge of the board.

15   Kf3-e4

White sees Black's plan, so he tries to keep his king in the center.

15   ...   Rh6-h2

For Black's plan to work, his rooks need to operate at a safe distance from the White king.

16   Qf8-g8

By attacking the rook on h7, White prevents Black from moving the other rook off the h-file.

16   ...   Rh7-d7

Black seizes control of the d-file and starts the process of herding the White king to the edge of the board. His plan is to gradually push the king toward the h-file.

17   Ke4-e3

Black's idea was to play Rh2-e2 check, pushing the king to the f-file. White tries to prevent the plan by guarding the e2-square. Now Black has to find another way.

| 17 | ... | a6-a5 |
| 18 | Qg8-e6 | Rh2-h7 |

By lining up the rooks on the seventh rank, Black can force his other rook to the e-file, pushing the king towards the edge.

| 19 | Qe6-g8 |

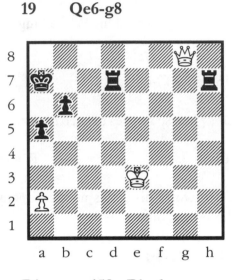

Diagram 152: Black to move

| 19 | ... | Rh7-e7 check |

United, the rooks can push the king to the f-file.

| 20 | Ke3-f3 | Rd7-d3 check |

This check will push the king to either f4 or f2.

| 21 | Kf3-f4 |

White is trying to keep his king away from the edges of the board. Hence, he steers his king toward the center for as long as possible.

21	...	Rd3-d1

Black is aiming to play Rd1-f1 check next turn, which will push the king over to the g-file.

22	Qg8-c4

White guards against the threat by moving the queen to c4, where it guards the f1 square.

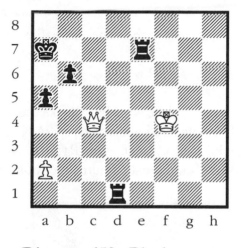

Diagram 153: Black on move

22	...	Rd1-f1 check!

But Black has a surprise! By noticing a tactical trick, Black's able to keep his plan on track. In this case, the tactical trick is called a skewer: If White now captures the audacious rook with 23 Qc4xf1, Black takes advantage of the lineup of White's king and queen on the same file and plays 23 ... Re7-f7 check! followed by 24 ... Rf7xf1.

With a rook to the good, Black would force checkmate easily.

Making progress in endings isn't just a matter of knowing grand strategical plans. You'll also need an alert eye for tactics like this, to push your plan forward at critical moments.

23   Kf4-g5

The White king is being forced even closer to the edge of the board.

23   ...   Re7-g7 check!

This pushes the king right to the edge, the h-file.

24   Kg5-h6

A good move. He reaches the edge but attacks the Black rook at the same time. If White had instead moved 24 Kg5-h4?, Black could have checkmated at once with Rf1-h1. Now if Black checks on h1, White's king just captures the rook on g7.

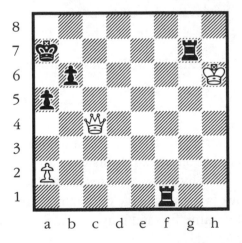

Diagram 154: Black on move

| 24 | ... | Rf1-g1 |

Both Black rooks were under attack, so he pauses for a second to consolidate his gains. With the king on the edge of the board, Black needs to regroup his rooks for a mating attack.

| 25 | Qc4-d4 |

White centers his queen and attacks the Black rook on g7.

There's no real threat here. Notice that even if White captures on g7 (26 Qd4xg7 Rg1xg7 27 Kh6xg7), White's king is too far away to stop the Black pawns. Black would just play b6-b5! and eventually queen one of his pawns. That's why it was so important for Black to pick up all the White pawns at the beginning of the ending. Any endgames that might result from trading off the major pieces are now lost for White.

| 25 | ... | Rg1-g4 |

Hoping White will fall into the trap of exchanging pieces.

| 26 | Qd4-d8 |

White sees the trap and just tries to keep his queen active.

26	...	Rg4-g6 check
27	Kh6-h5	Rg6-g2
28	Kh5-h6	

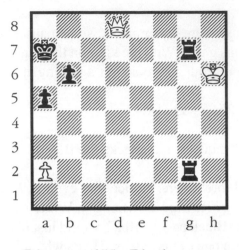

Diagram 155: Black on move

Black's plan has stalled a bit. Although White's king is on the edge of the board, it's the wrong edge. As long as Black's rook on g7 is tied to the seventh rank (to prevent White from starting an infinite series of checks on the Black king), Black can't make any more progress. White will keep attacking the rook with his king, and Black's other rook will be tied down to protecting the one on g7.

The solution is to somehow chase the White king to the eighth rank (the top edge of the board). Then Black's rooks on the seventh rank will simultaneously protect the Black king while launching checkmating threats against the White king. How is that to be accomplished? Let's watch Reshevsky pull it off.

28 ...   **Rg7-b7!**

The rook gets away from the White king, but still keeps a grip on the seventh rank to prevent checks to the Black king.

29 **Qd8-d5**

Attacking the rook on g2.

29	...	Rg2-c2!

Black's idea is to operate against the White king using the ranks (horizontal rows), rather than the files (vertical rows). Black is also taking advantage of the fact that his pawn on b6 controls the c5 square. Now if White tries to get his king back to the center by 30 Kh6-g5?, Black will play 30 ... Rc2-c5!, pinning the White queen to the king. (Those tactical ideas again!)

30	Qd5-b3

The queen gets out of the rook's way.

30	...	Rc2-c5!

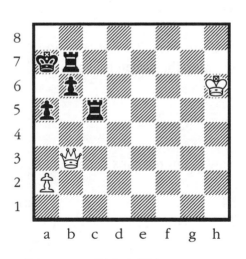

Diagram 156: White on move

Take a look. By repositioning his rooks, Black has sandwiched the White king to the sixth rank. The next job is to push it to the seventh.

31 Qb3-e3

The best White can do is to keep his queen centered, trying to counter Black's maneuvers as they develop.

31 ...   Rb7-d7

Now Black threatens 32 ... Rd7-d6 check followed by Rc5-c7 check, pushing the king to the eighth row. White has to counter this plan or he's cooked.

32 Qe3-e6!

The queen guards the d6 square, temporarily stopping Black's plan.

32 ...   Rd7-c7

Black switches to a new idea: Rc7-c6, pinning the White queen to the king and winning the queen for a rook. White must move the queen to safety.

33 Qe6-e4

The queen steps away but remains centralized.

34 ...   Rc7-c6 check
35 Kh6-g7

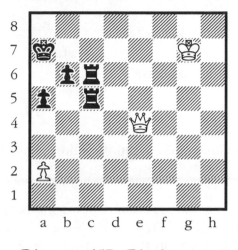

Diagram 157: Black on move

Black has made some progress. The White king is now on the seventh rank, just one row away from the target, the eighth rank. But how does Black consolidate his gains? He'd like to leave his rook on c6, keeping the White king where it is, and maneuver the other rook to give check somewhere on the seventh rank. That would push White to the eighth. Unfortunately, the rook on c5 needs to stay where it is to guard the rook on c6. And if the rook on c6 moves back to c7, then the White king skips back to the sixth rank. How can Black untangle his rooks to make further progress?

| 35 | ... | Ka7-b7! |

The Black king has to do its part. By guarding the rook on c6, he frees the other rook for offensive maneuvers. And notice that with White's king now on the seventh rank, Black doesn't have to worry about checks anymore. If White tries 36 Qe4-e7 check??, Black replies 36 ... Rc6-c7, pinning the queen to her own king!

| 36 | Kg7-f7 | Rc5-h5! |

273

The freed rook jumps into action: Rh5-h7 check!

37   Kf7-g7

Stops that threat for the moment.

37   ...   Rh5-h6!

Black has a new threat: 38 ... Rh6-d6 followed by 39 ... Rd6-d7 check.

As before, White has the opportunity to win both opposing rooks for his own queen. He could play 38 Qe4-e7 check Rc6-c7 39 Qe7xc7 check Kb7xc7 40 Kg7xh6. However, his king would still be too far away from Black's pawns, and Black would play b6-b5! and eventually queen a pawn.

38   Kg7-f8

White couldn't stop the threat, but by leaving his queen on e4, he prevents either of the Black rooks from moving to the seventh rank. The queen guards h7 and pins the other rook.

38   ...   Rh6-h8 check!

This check does the trick for Black. By forcing the king back to the seventh rank, Black sets up another tactical trick.

39   Kf8-e7

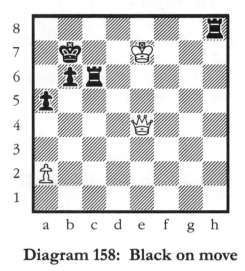

Diagram 158: Black on move

| 39 | ... | Rh8-h7 check! |

Here's the idea. If White captures the rook by Qe4xh7, Black has another skewer: Rc6-c7 check followed by Rc7xh7. Once again, Black makes progress by seeing more deeply into the tactics of the position.

| 40 | Ke7-d8 | |

Now White is trapped on the eighth rank — permanently. Black's job now is to work out a checkmating maneuver. First he has to coordinate his rooks again.

| 41 | ... | Rh7-c7 |

This guards the c6 rook, which enables the king to move, thus unpinning the rook and letting the rook move. Once Black unties the knot, both rooks will be active, and White will be finished.

| 42 | Qe4-d5 | Kb7-a7 |

Now the rook at c6 is free to move.

| 43 | Qd5-e5 | Rc7-b7! |

The rook slips away from the White king's attack allowing the other rook to move to the seventh rank.

| 44 | Qe5-g5 | Rc6-b7! |

With two rooks lined up on the seventh rank, Black can generate multiple checkmating threats.

| 45 | Qg5-e5 |

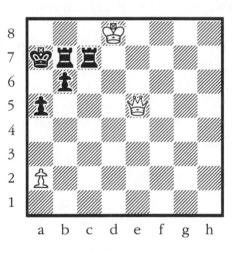

Diagram 159: Black on move

| 46 | ... | Rc7-h7 |

The end of a long road. Black's first threat is 47 ... Rb7-b8 check, which forces White to give up his queen to stop mate. If White prevents this threat by playing 47 Kd7-c7, Black just plays 47 ... Rh7-h8 check! 48 Qe5xh8 Rb7-b8 check, followed by 49 ... Rb8xh8. Either way, Black ends up a rook ahead, so

White finally gives up.

Using the King

In the next ending, White's problem is a little more difficult.

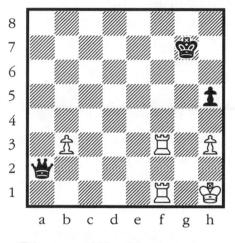

Diagram 160: Black on move

On the plus side, White has two rooks against a queen, plus an extra pawn. That would normally be enough of an advantage for an easy win. On the downside, he has only two remaining pawns, on opposite sides of the board. That means his king lacks any permanent, safe haven from Black's queen checks.

To win the game, White will have to advance his king into the middle of the board with his rooks, and use it as a fighting piece to help his pawns advance. Along the way, he'll pick off Black's h-pawn at some point to give himself two passed pawns. It's a plan which requires ingenuity and patience, but it can be done, and we'll show you how.

This ending arose from a recent game between Anatoly Karpov and Viswanathan Anand. Karpov took over the World Championship when Bobby Fischer retired in 1975, and held it for ten years, until he was defeated by Garry Kasparov. He remains one of the world's top five players for a long time. His play is careful and accurate; at his best, he exploits small positional advantages with great precision, slowly squeezing his opponents until their positions collapse. Anand is the finest player ever to emerge from India, and he is also currently rated one of the world's top-five. In 1995, he lost a close match for the World Championship to Kasparov.

1	...	Qa2-c2

Black's queen is a little offside in the position (he just captured a White pawn on a2) so Black prepares to centralize it.

2	Rf1-f2!

The two rooks now provide cover for the White king to enter the game via g2 and g3. Remember, the king will have to be a fighting piece in this ending, since it has no hiding places in the corners of the board.

It might seem incredible that a king can venture out into the middle of an open board when the opponent has a queen and plenty of room to maneuver. But as we'll see, two rooks can guard a lot of squares.

2	...	Qc2-e4

Checks don't necessarily do any good. After 2 ... Qc2-d1 check 3 Kh1-g2, Black is already out of checks. If Black tries 2 ... Qc2-b1 check 3 Kh1-g2 Qb1-g6 check??, White wins immediately with 4 Rf3-g3!, pinning the queen. Instead, Black just pins the front rook. His strategy is just to be as much of a nuisance as possible, putting obstacles in White's path and hoping for a blunder.

3   Kh1-g2

The king begins marching to the center.

3   ...   Qe4-b4

The queen blocks the b-pawn while preventing the White king from crossing the fourth rank.

4   Rf2-e2

One point of this move is to opens a path for the White king to advance, via f2. The more important point is to reposition this rook in front of the rook on f3, controlling more space. (The f3 rook can't move for now without losing the b-pawn.)

4   ...   Qb4-d4

Guards the f2-square, preventing the White king from marching that way.

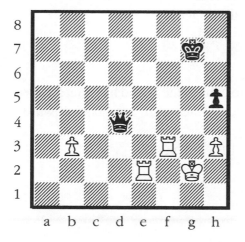

Diagram 161: White on move

5	Re2-e7 check	Kg7-g6
6	Re7-e6 check	Kg6-g7
7	Rf3-g3 check	Kg7-f7
8	Rg3-e3!	

This was White's idea all along — to reposition his rooks so that one rook controls the sixth rank while the other, from e3, guards both pawns. Now the White king can advance into the center of the board.

| 8 | ... | Qd4-d5 check |

Black will still try to disrupt White's plans by giving check whenever possible. Unfortunately, the White rooks control most of the key squares on the board.

| 9 | Kg2-g3 |

The king heads toward the center. Depending on how Black plays, White's king can take one of several routes: Kg3-f4-e5 or Kg3-h4xh5, or Kg3-f2-e2-d3. Black can block some of these routes but not all of them.

| 9 | ... | Qd5-g5 check |

Black decides to control the f4 and h4 squares, saving his h-pawn at the same time. White has to head back toward f2.

| 10 | Kg3-f2 |

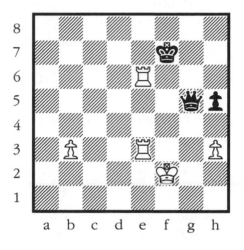

Diagram 162: Black on move

10	...	Qg5-h4 check

Not the best square for the queen (on the side of the board and blocked in by pawns) but it's the only check available. Notice that if Black plays 10 ... Qg5-f5 check or Qg5-f4 check, White replies with 11 Re3-f3!, pinning the Black queen against the Black king. That doesn't win the queen outright, since Black would play 11 ... Qxf3 check 12 Kf2xf3 Kf7xe6, trading the queen for two rooks. Unfortunately for Black, though, the king and pawn ending would be hopelessly lost. White would advance his b-pawn as a decoy, driving the Black king over to the b-file, then capture Black's h-pawn with his king, eventually queening his own h-pawn.

One of White's hidden strengths in this endgame is that all king and pawn endings are won for him in just that way, so Black has to be very careful about aligning his king and queen on the same rank or file. That's another way in which Black's checking possibilities are severely limited.

> ### 11   Kf2-e2

The king heads for d3 and points north and west.

> ### 11   ...   Qh4-d4

The queen had totally run out of checks, so she blocks the king from moving to the d-file.

> ### 12   Re6-e4!

White can't be too rigid about where he places his rooks. The ideal formation may well be on e3 and e6, but he will still have to maneuver to force his king forward.

> ### 12   ...   Qd4-a1

Black has to decide whether he wants to allow the White king to penetrate the queenside or the kingside. If Black checks on b2, the White king moves to f3 and then f4, threatening the pawn on h5. Black decides to prevent this maneuvering by going to a1, preparing to move to f1 if necessary. However, this allows the White king into d3 and then c4. Black can only prevent one line of attack: he decides that saving his h-pawn is top priority for now.

> ### 13   Ke2-d3   Kf7-f6

Checks don't help. They just drive the White king where he wants to go. The queen is well-placed, keeping the White king out of c3 and d4, so Black improves the position of his king.

> ### 14   Re4-e6 check

White resumes the preferred placing of his rooks, on e6 and e3, where they guard many of the critical squares the queen will need to access to give perpetual check.

	14	...		Kf6-f5

There's no future for the king at f7. From f5 he's ready to guard the h-pawn.

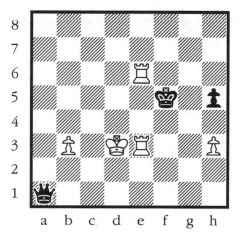

Diagram 163: White on move

	15	b3-b4!

White starts the next phase of his plan. Now that his king is centered, he's going to move the pawn from b3 to b6 where it will be guarded by the front rook. On the intermediate squares, b4 and b5, the king will take over the job of guarding the pawn.

	15	...		Qa1-c1

Cuts the White king off from the b-file. Checks don't help, as they just force the king to c4, where he wants to go anyway.

16	Kd3-d4	

Now White is ready to push the pawn on to b5 next turn.

16	...	Qc1-c8

Still keeping the king off the c-file.

17	b4-b5!	

Now the pawn can't be stopped from reaching b6.

17	...	Qc8-d8 check

Since he can't stop the pawn, Black decides to give a few checks.

18	Kd4-c5	Qd8-c7 check
19	Kc5-b4	Qc7-f4 check
20	Kb4-b3!	

As we learned in the last chapter, the best way to avoid checks is to keep the king on a square of the opposite color from the one the enemy queen is on. This eliminates checks along most of the diagonals.

Now Black is out of checks again. Take a look at the next diagram, in which the squares controlled by the White pieces and pawns are marked with an 'x':

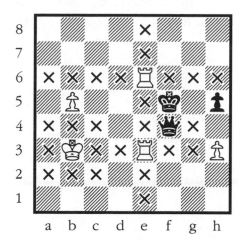

Diagram 164: 'x' Marks the squares that white controls

The diagram makes Black's problem clear. The only areas of the board where the queen can freely move to give check are off in the corners. White controls almost the whole center section with his pieces. Instead of a powerful piece controlling the flow of events, Black's queen is more like a hunted fugitive, taking pot shots from long-range.

20   ...   Qf4-c7

There's no future over on the king-side, so Black repositions the queen to at least prevent the pawn from moving to b7.

21   b5-b6!

Mission accomplished. The pawn sits well-protected, just two squares from queening.

21   ...   Qc7-d7

Again, from a Black square the queen has no checks, so Black repositions the queen to a White square. Now some checking possibilities open up (b5, d5, and d1).

22   Re3-e5 check

With the pawn now safe at b6, White decides to check for awhile with his rooks, to see where Black will place his king.

22   ...   Kf5-f4

A forced play.

23   Re5-e4 check   Kf4-g3

Not a good idea. Black had nothing better than Kf4-f5, repeating the position. Black's move looks aggressive, but now his king gets cut off from his own h-pawn.

24   Re4-e3 check   Kg3-h2

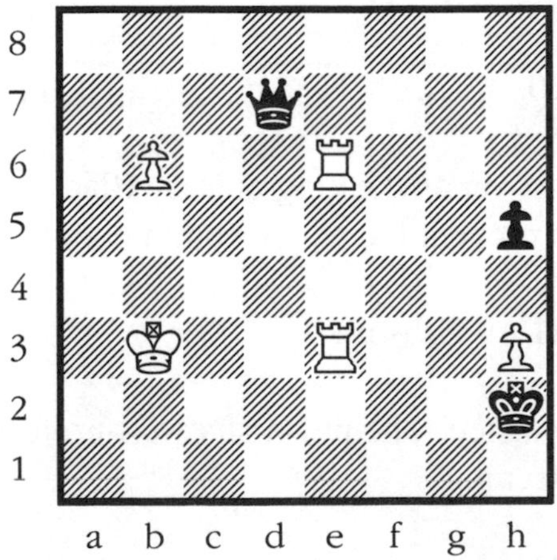

Diagram 165: White on move

Black's king is stuck in the corner, trapped by White's rook at e3. White now embarks on a new plan. With the Black king cut off, White's own king heads toward the Black pawn.

25   Kb3-c4!

The pawn will prove very hard to defend with a White king in the vicinity.

25   ...   h5-h4

No need to move the queen, which right now is preventing the king from crossing the d-file. Meanwhile, the pawn is just as safe here as on h5.

26   Kc4-c5

To get to the king-side, White will have to operate with double threats. Now White is threatening Re6-e7, followed by the advance of the b-pawn.

26   ...   Qd7-c8 check

Chases the king away from the c5-c6 area. The b-pawn is White's most dangerous threat, so the Black queen has to keep an eye on it.

27   Kc5-d5!

A move like 27 Re6-c6, blocking the check, might look tempting, but Black would reply with 27 ... Qc8-f5 check, and with his rooks disconnected, White would have to be very careful. After 28 Kc5-d6, for instance, Black would have a double attack with 28 ... Qf5-f4 check!, and after 29 Re3-e5 (the only move to save the rook), Black would gobble a pawn with 29 ... Kh2xh3.

Keeping the rooks connected until the right moment is the surest way to win.

27	...	Qc8-d8 check
28	Kd5-e4!	

The king heads for h4 and the Black pawn. Again, staying on a square of the opposite color from the Black queen's square minimizes the checks.

28	...	Qd8-d7

Stops the b-pawn from moving.

29	Ke4-f5

Continues on track toward the h-pawn.

29	...	Kh2-g2

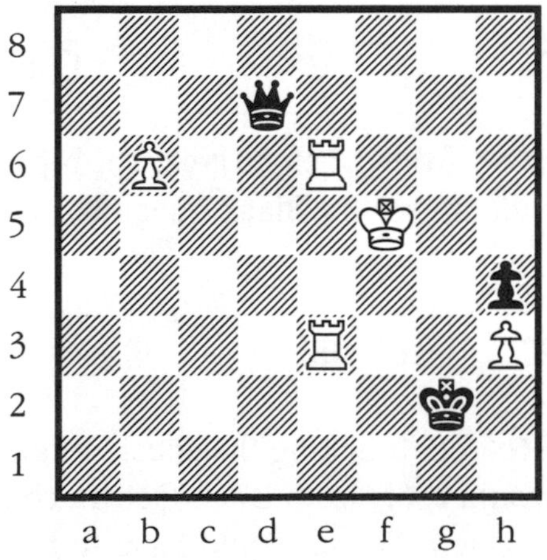

Diagram 166: White on move

30	Kf5-g5

Finally White attacks the h-pawn.

30	...	Qd7-g7 check

Black could defend the pawn with 30 ... Qd7-h7, but the queen would be left out of play. White would reply with 31 Kg5-g4! and suddenly Black would be facing mating threats. White would be ready to play 32 Re3-e2 check Kg2-f1 33 Re2-e1 check Kf1-f2 34 Re6-e2 checkmate. Black could move his queen and prevent the checkmate, but he'd have to give up the pawn anyway.

31	Kg5xh4	Kg2-f2

Hoping to play to f3 if White checks on e2.

32	Re3-e5

There's no need to keep the rook on the third rank any longer. With the Black pawn eliminated, White doesn't have to worry about protecting his own h-pawn. (White's b-pawn is enough to win the game.) The next job is to get the king back toward the queenside.

32	...	Qg7-h8 check

Black tries to keep the king busy with checks.

| 33 | Kh4-g4 | Qh8-g7 check |
| 34 | Kg4-f5 | Qg7-h7 check |

Diagram 167: White on move

35   Kf5-f6!

White sees that he doesn't need to guard the h-pawn, because it's indirectly protected by tactics. If Black now plays 35 ... Qh7xh3, the sequence is 36 Re5-e2 check Kf2-f1 37 Re2-e1 check Kf1-f2 38 Re6-e2 check Kf2-g3 39 Re2-e3 check! winning the queen with a skewer. So White just keeps pushing his king forward. Noticing these tactical tricks can make the difference between winning a tough game or settling for a draw.

35   ...   Qh7-h4 check

Black sees White's trap, and continues his checks.

36   Kf6-f7

Heading for e8 and the queenside. But another new possibility has opened up, which White might be able to exploit instead. His rooks can now operate against the Black king on the files.

290

For instance, if it were White's move now, he could play 37 Re5-f5 check Kf2-g2 38 Re6-g6 check Kg2-h2. This sequence wouldn't lead to checkmate (yet) but it would force the Black king in the corner, and it's definitely an idea to keep in mind for the future.

Always be prepared to revise your original game plan when new ideas open up.

36	...	Qh4-h7 check
37	Kf7-e8	Qh7-b7

If Black grabs the h-pawn, White wins with the maneuver Re5-e2 check, Re2-e1 check, and Re6-e2 check, as we noticed before. But there's now another reason for leaving the h-pawn on the board: it provides Black's king with some much-needed cover from the rampaging White rooks.

38	h3-h4!

On the other hand, by not taking the pawn, Black leaves White the option to just march this pawn up the board as well. Since it doesn't disturb the position, White might as well march this pawn as far as it goes.

38	...	Qb7-b8 check
39	Ke8-f7	Qb8-b7 check
40	Kf7-g6	

Diagram 168: Black on move

White controls so much of the board that Black runs out of checks very quickly. If Black now plays his last check, 40 ... Qb7-g2 check, White has 41 Kg6-f6! and there are no more checks. (41 ... Qg2-f3 check is answered by 42 Re5-f5! pinning the Black queen.)

40	...	Qb7-b8

Black aims for Qb8-g8 check, which keeps the queen in play and continues to guard against the advance of the b-pawn.

41	h4-h5

The advance of the h-pawn opens a second front. The pawns are now equally threatening.

41	...	Qb8-g8 check

Keeping White busy is all Black can do.

42	Kg6-f5	Qg8-h7 check

This is the right checking square. If Black checks on f8, White blocks with 43 Re6-f6! and then when White's king next moves, it will be with a discovered check. For example, 42 ... Qg8-f8 check 43 Re6-f6 Qf8-c8 check 44 Kf5-g6 discovered check Kf2-g2 45 Re5-g5 check, and Black's king is in serious trouble.

43	Kf5-f6!	

Black's only checks now are from h8 or h6, and those aren't ideal squares for the queen. Black wants to keep the queen as centralized as possible, else the queen runs out of checks too quickly.

43	...	Kf2-f3!

Sometimes the best defense lies in doing nothing. Right now neither White pawn can advance and the king can't move forward either, so Black just bides time with his king.

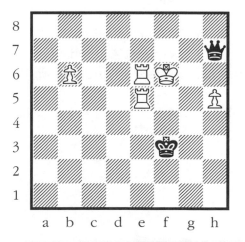

Diagram 169: White on move

44	Re5-e3 check

White's a little stuck in his current formation, so he starts to rearrange his rooks.

44	...	Kf3-f2
45	Kf6-g5	Qh7-g8 check
46	Kg5-h4	Qg8-d8 check

Black's only check.

| 47 | Kh4-h3 |

By moving toward the Black king, White has eliminated many of Black's checks while opening up some checkmating possibilities.

| 47 | ... | Qd8-d1? |

Black is trying to get to h1 for a check, but he overlooks a maneuver by White that finishes the game off immediately.

| 48 | Re3-e2 check! |

If Black now moves to f1, White plays Re2-e1 check! and trades his two rooks for Black's queen. After that he can queen either or both of his pawns. So Black's replay is forced.

| 48 | ... | Kf2-f3 |
| 49 | Re2-e1! |

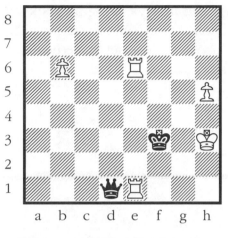

Diagram 170: Black resigns

With the rooks both separated from the Black king, White has two deadly threats, Re6-f6 check or Re1-f1 check, which will either be checkmate or will win Black's queen for a rook. Black gives up. A great ending by Karpov!

Drawing with the Queen

The two rooks don't always beat a queen. Sometimes the queen can hold its own or even win. In order to survive or even triumph, the queen needs to be able to prevent cooperation between the two rooks. Here are some of the factors that help the queen:

More pawns. This is a curious asset, since, as we have learned, the usual rule in endings is that the weaker side tries to trade pawns and get down to an ending with no pawns on the board at all. That strategy doesn't work well in a situation where the queen faces two rooks, since as the pawns go off the board, the rooks wreak havoc on the wide-open lines. The presence of a lot of pawns can jam up the rook's activity.

Weak pawns. A single weak pawn might require tying up a whole rook to defend it, effectively cutting the rook's power in half. Weak king position. If the side with the rooks has an exposed king, the queen may be able to set up perpetual check threats.

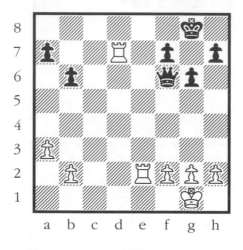

Diagram 171: Black on move

In Diagram 171, White seems to be doing well. The pawns are even, and his two rooks control the two center files. White is even threatening Rd7xa7 or Re2-e7, both of which look like winning moves. However, Black can take advantage of the factors mentioned above to generate just enough counterplay to save the game. Let's watch and see how he does it.

| 1 | ... | Qf6-c6! |

A good move with a double threat: Qc6xd7 and Qc6-c1 check followed by mate. White has to defend against the checkmate; he doesn't have time to rip off the pawn on a7.

| 2 | Rd7-d1 |

Meets the threat, at the cost of being pushed on the defensive, at least temporarily.

2	...	g6-g5!

Good chess is about anticipation. The best formation of pawns for guarding the White king is pawns on f2-g3-h4, with the king tucked away on h2. From that position, and as long as the pawn on f2 is defended somehow by a rook, no checks are possible, and the pawns all guard each other. Black understands this, so he takes immediate measures to make sure that White will have to settle for a weaker, less desireable formation by preventing the White pawn from reaching h4.

3	h2-h3

White has to create some air space for his king so that the rook on d1 is free to roam.

3	...	Kg8-g7

The king avoids any checks and gets closer to the action.

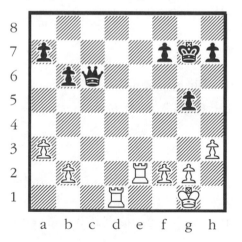

Diagram 172: White on move

4	b2-b4

White grabs more space on the queenside, but now the a3-pawn could come under attack. The pawns on b2 and f2 only required one rook to defend them both. Pawns on a3 and f2 could be tougher to defend.

4   ...   Kg7-g6

The king gets ready to play an active role in opening up the kingside. Black needs to open lines to the White king to set up a possible perpetual check.

5   g2-g3

White has now created a safe spot at h2 for his king.

5   ...   h7-h5!

No sooner has White created a haven than Black tries to blast it open. Now he's ready to proceed with h5-h4 or g5-g4, as the occasion warrants.

6   Re2-e7

White decides that his king's position is as safe as it can be, so he sends a rook after the a7-pawn.

6   ...   f7-f6!

Black doesn't have enough pieces to tie them down to passive defense. Instead he shelters his king from checks along the sixth rank, and prepares a counter-attack if White sends his rook off to a7.

298

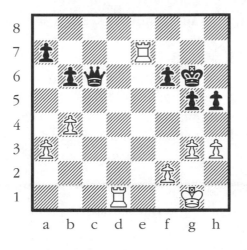

Diagram 173: White on move

Now White sees that his kingside could come under a strong attack if he captures the a-pawn with his rook. Here's a possible sequence. After 7 Re7xa7, Black would play 7 ... Qc6-f3! attacking the rook on d1 and the pawn on a3. Then after 8 Rd1-e1, h5-h4! starts to open up the kingside. After 9 Re1-e3 Qf3-d1 check 10 Kg1-h2 Qd1-f1, White appears to be able to guard everything with 11 Re3-f3. But Black can play 11 ... g5-g4!!, and after 12 h3xg4 h4-h3!!, White actually gets checkmated. This variation isn't forced, and White has other defensive tries, but it shows how dangerous the queen can be when the rooks are disconnected and only one remains to defend against a rampaging queen.

7	Re7-e3

White sees that he can get into trouble if he goes too far afield, so he drops back to try something else.

7	...	Kg6-g7

Black doesn't see a good way to improve his position at this point, so he plays a waiting move to see if White has a real plan.

8	g3-g4?

White comes up with a bad idea. This creates a pawn which is both weak and easily attacked — a bad combination. Now Black can get a solid draw by tying White's pieces down to defending this pawn.

8	...	h5xg4
9	h3xg4	Qc6-c4!

Black immediately moves to attack the pawn.

10	Re3-g3

The White rook guards both the pawn on g4 and the pawn on a3, but with one rook tied down, he doesn't have enough ammunition to make progress in other parts of the board.

10	...	Kg7-g6
11	Rd1-d3	Qc4-c1 check
12	Kg1-h2	Qc1-f4

Black doesn't have to do anything concrete to get his draw — it's enough just to make small threats and prevent White from doing anything.

13	Rd3-f3	Qf4-d6
14	Rf3-f5	a7-a6
15	Kh2-h1	Qd6-d1 check
16	Kh1-h2	

Here the game was given up as a draw. White can't make any progress as long as one of his rooks was tied to the defense of the g4-pawn.

Moral: The rooks don't look powerful when they're tied down defending weak pawns. To assert their superiority, the rooks need a wide-open board to roam.

Tactical Tricks

Not every ending requires long, drawn-out strategy to win. Sometimes you just have to be alert to tactical strokes that lie just below the surface of the position. Here are two amazing examples of what's possible when you stay alert, even if your opponent has a mighty queen.

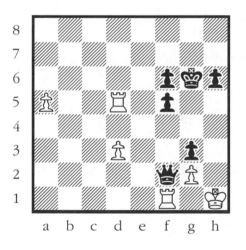

Diagram 174: White on move

White looks to be in some trouble in Diagram 174. Black has just played his queen to f2, attacking the White rook. Obviously White can't capture the queen, since Black would play g3xf2, and the pawn would queen next turn. But if White moves his rook away, say with Rf1-b1, Black plays f5-f4!, and threatens to push on to f3 next turn, with checkmating threats.

301

What's White to do?

Answer: stay alert and look at all legal checks and captures! When former World Champion Alexander Alekhine encountered this, he found his way clear to an easy win with some tactical alertness. Here's how he played:

1	Rf1xf2!!

Incredible. How can White stop the f2 pawn from queening?

1	...	g3xf2

Now what?

2	Rd5xf5!!

This stops the pawn for one turn. But there's a subtle point.

2	...	Kg6xf5
3	g2-g4 check!	

The final twist. White moves the g2-pawn with a tempo check, clearing the way for his king to get to g2.

3	...	Kf5xg4
4	Kh1-g2	

The White king stops the pawn. Now his own pawn at a5 will queen before Black can get his h-pawn moving. Brilliant!

Alekhine strikes again in this next neat endgame maneuver:

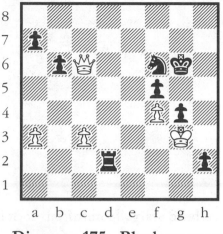

Diagram 175: Black on move

This time the White queen faces a Black rook a Black knight. Black also has a strong passed pawn, ready to queen. But White has the queening square under guard. If Black moves the rook off the second rank, White will play Kg3xh2. Meanwhile, the Black knight is pinned by the White queen. (A good thing, since otherwise Black would win by Nf6-e4 check.) Unpinning the knight looks difficult. If Black retreats his king, White will start checking with his queen on c7 or b7. If Black evades the checks by going back to the sixth rank, White will move his queen back to c6 with another pin. Does Alekhine have a winning idea? He does, and it's quite a nice one.

1   ...   Kg6-h5!

Black abandons the pinned knight and walks into a checkmating net. Method, or madness?

2   Qc6xf6

Now if Black queens his pawn, White plays Qf6-g5 checkmate.

2   ...   h2-h1 (N) checkmate!

Diagram 176: White is checkmated

Black underpromotes to a knight, and White gets checkmated first. Stay alert — it pays!

16. NEXT STEPS

You've seen the power of an aggressive, centralized king, the need to create a passed pawn and use it as a diversion, and the necessity for tactical alertness to make progress in apparently blocked positions. You've also noticed the importance of precise calculation.

As you practice, don't be content with reading or playing against your local circle of friends. Try to locate clubs or tournaments in your area where you can meet new people and play in organized competitions. You'll meet folks who share your interests, and you'll improve much faster.

Keep reading, keep playing, and keep winning!